W9-CLQ-525

The Singular Life Story of
Heedless Hopalong

Frontispiece from the 1683 edition of Grimmelshausen's *Simplicissimi*
... *Buch von dem seltzamen Springinsfeld*. The inscription reads:
Behold mad Hopalong at play!
He plays the fool in every way.
How like our madcap world today!

THE SINGULAR LIFE STORY OF HEEDLESS HOPALONG

Hans Jacob Christoffel von Grimmelshausen

Translated and Annotated by
Robert L. Hiller and John C. Osborne

Wayne State University Press
Detroit 1981

Library of Congress Cataloging in Publication Data

Grimmelshausen, Hans Jakob Christoph von, 1625-1676.
The singular life story of heedless Hopalong.

Translation of: Der Seltzame Springinsfeld.
Bibliography: p.
1. Thirty Years' War, 1618-1648—Fiction.
I. Hiller, Robert Ludwig, 1915-   II. Osborne,
John G., 1928-   III. Title.
PT1731.S7E5   1981   833'.5   81-10446
ISBN 0-8143-1688-3   AACR2

Grateful acknowledgment is extended to the Yale Collection of German Literature, Beinecke Rare Book and Manuscript Library, Yale University, for permission to include illustrations from its 1683 edition of Hans Jacob Christoffel von
Grimmelshausen's *Simplicissimi . . . Buch von dem seltzamen Springinsfeld.*

*Recipient of the First
Basilius Award in Germanics*

Contents

THE SINGULAR LIFE STORY OF HEEDLESS HOPALONG
by Philarcho Grosso von Tromerheim, Anno 1670

Chronology of Grimmelshausen's Works*

Note: included for each work is the German short title, the nom de plume *(in parentheses), and the English short title (in brackets).*

1666   *Satyrischer Pilgram I* (Samuel Greifnson vom Hirschfeld), [*The Satirical Pilgrim, Part I*]

       Der keusche Joseph (Samuel Greifnson von Hirschfeld), [*Chaste Joseph*]

1667   *Satyrischer Pilgram II* (Samuel Greifnson vom Hirschfeld), [*The Satirical Pilgrim, Part II*]

1668   *Simplicissimus* I–V (German Schleifheim von Sulsfort), [*Simplicissimus*]

1669   *Die Continuatio* [*Simplicissimus* VI] (German Schleifheim von Sulsfort), [*Continuatio*]

1670   *Dietwald und Amelinde* (H. J. Christoffel von Grimmelshausen), [*Dietwald and Amelinde*]

       Ratio Status (Hans Jacob Christoph von Grimmelshausen), [*Ratio Status*]

       Landstörtzerin Courasche (Philarchus Grossus von Trommenheim), [*Runagate Courage*]

       Der seltzame Springinsfeld (Philarchus Grossus von Tromerheim), [*Heedless Hopalong*]

       Der erste Beernhäuter (Illiteratus Ignorantius), [*The First Sluggard*]

*Not listed are the various *Europäische Wundergeschichten-Calender* [*European Calender of Wondrous Stories*], the authorship of which is now disputed.

Simplicissimi Gauckeltasche (Illiteratus Ignorantius), [*The Simplicissimi Magic Book*]

Musai (Samuel Greifnson von Hirschfeld), [*Musai*]

1671   *Der ewigwährende Calender* (Simplicissimus), [*The Perpetual Calendar*]

1672   *Rathstübl Plutonis* (Erich Stainfels von Grufensholm), [*Plutus' Council Chamber*]

Die verkehrte Welt (Simon Lengfrisch vom Hartenfels), [*The Topsy-Turvy World*]

Proximus und Lympida (H. J. Christoffel von Grimmelshausen), [*Proximus and Lympida*]

Das wunderbarliche Vogelnest I (Michael Rechulin von Sehmsdorff), [*The Wondrous Bird's Nest, Part I*]

Der stoltze Melcher (no author given), [*Proud Melcher*]

1673   *Der Teutsche Michel* (Signeur Messmal), [*German Michel*]

Der Bartkrieg (no author given), [*The War of the Beards*]

Das Galgen-Männlin (Israel Fromschmidt von Hugenfelss), [*The Mandrake*]

1675   *Das wunderbarliche Vogelnest II* (Aceeeffghhiillmmnnoorrssstuu), [*The Wondrous Bird's Nest, Part II*]

Preface

The Singular Life Story of Heedless Hopalong is the third of the
five novels by Hans Jacob Christoffel von Grimmelshausen which make
up the so-called Simplician cycle. The first, longest, and best-known
novel of the cycle, *Simplicissimus*, has long been recognized by critics
as the first great German novel and has been available in English translation for some time. Our own English rendering of the second of the
Simplician novels, *The Runagate Courage,* appeared fifteen years ago,
and its favorable reception by the public and by critics encouraged us to
turn to the next novel in the cycle. *The Singular Life Story of Heedless
Hopalong* presents for the first time a complete and annotated English
version of the first edition of *Der seltzame Springinsfeld* (several
chapters from it appeared as an appendix to our *The Runagate Courage*
and are reprinted with the kind permission of the University of Nebraska
Press).

With the appearance of *Heedless Hopalong* three of the five Simplician novels are now available in English translation. Within the next
few years we hope to complete annotated scholarly translations of the
remaining two works in the cycle, *The Wondrous Bird's Nest, Part I*
and *The Wondrous Bird's Nest, Part II,* thereby making accessible to
English-speaking readers the entire Simplician cycle, one of the most
significant and delightful group of prose fiction works in world literature.

Behold our valiant Hopalong,
The captive of a ravening throng,
'Til friendly troopers come along.

Translators' Note

Heedless Hopalong is based primarily on J. H. Scholte's edition of the first edition (1670) of Grimmelshausen's *Der seltzame Springinsfeld,* but the texts and notes of a number of other editions were consulted (see Bibliography, Part A). In order to preserve as much as possible the flavor of the German original, we have chosen, as we did in our translation of *Die Landstörtzerin Courasche (The Runagate Courage,* Lincoln, Nebraska: University of Nebraska Press, 1965), to leave most of the many foreign words and phrases in the text untranslated, and to retain the "Baroque" sentence structure and rhetorical flourishes whenever they do not obscure the meaning. Even though in virtually all instances the meaning of the foreign words and phrases should be obvious from the context or from English cognates, a list of them and their English equivalents precedes the text.

The vagaries of seventeenth-century spelling of proper names have been retained in the Chronology of Grimmelshausen's Works, the main text, the Notes, and the Bibliography. Thus there may be several variations in the spelling of a single name in each.

Notes to the text, arranged by chapter, are appended. A list of the short titles of the secondary works cited precedes the Notes. References to works by Grimmelshausen are given by book and chapter, so that any edition may be consulted. All translations from German in the Notes are our own.

Behold how Hopalong shows anew:
That fortune is fickle is all too true.
He fights and wins, but loses too.

Introduction

When Grimmelshausen's *The Singular Life Story of Heedless Hopalong*, ostensibly written by Philarchus Grossus von Tromerheim, first appeared in late 1670 or early 1671, it was as nearly guaranteed of commercial success as any work of fiction can be. Its titular hero and primary narrator was already familiar to the German reading public as a minor character in the most popular novel of the age, *Simplicissimus*, and as a major character in its sequel, *The Runagate Courage*.

Simplicissimus, which presumably first appeared at the Spring Book Fair in Frankfurt in 1668, went through five editions; at least two of these were reprinted. The work was such a success that Grimmelshausen and other authors were quick to capitalize on it by producing books which were supposed to have been written either by Simplicius Simplicissimus or by one of the Simplician characters, or which mentioned "Simplicissimus" or "Simplician" prominently in the title. By 1675 fifteen such works had appeared; by 1700 at least fifteen more.

Of these many works, only five, all by Hans Jacob Christoffel von Grimmelshausen, make up the so-called "Simplician Cycle": the original novel, *Simplicissimus* (in six volumes), and its successors, *The Runagate Courage, The Singular Life Story of Heedless Hopalong, The Wondrous Bird's Nest, Part I*, and *The Wondrous Bird's Nest, Part II*. Indeed, the novels of the Simplician cycle are links in a chain; beginning with the second one, *Courage*, each arises from the preceding work.

In *Simplicissimus* the titular hero-narrator describes his life from his birth on June 22, 1622, the date of the Battle of Höchst in the Thirty

Years' War (1618–48), to about his forty-fifth year. One of his adventures concerns a "beautiful lady" whom he met at a spa, seduced, and then got rid of through "the scurviest trick." Another series of episodes describe his exploits as a famous soldier, "the huntsman of Soest," and in these his chief accomplice is an uncouth veteran soldier named Hopalong.

The Runagate Courage, the second novel in the cycle, purports to be the autobiography of Courage, the nameless "beautiful lady" of *Simplicissimus.* When Courage learns that Simplicissimus has publicly shamed her by telling how he jilted her, she becomes so angry that she takes revenge by telling her own life story. Thus, *The Runagate Courage* is to show the world "what kind of honorable minx he [Simplicissimus] was dealing with, so that he may know of what he bragged and may perhaps wish that he had kept silent." Courage relates how her lustiness, valor, and ill fortune provide her with one husband or lover after another until she decides to become a sutler (a seller of provisions to the army) and for that purpose takes as a common-law husband a young musketeer, who turns out to be none other than Simplicius Simplicissimus' comrade at Soest, Hopalong.

The third novel in the cycle, *The Singular Life Story of Heedless Hopalong,* presents Hopalong's life story and provides the basis for the last two novels in the cycle, *The Wondrous Bird's Nest, Part I* and *II.* Hopalong's last wife, the hurdy-gurdy girl, finds the nest, which makes its bearer invisible, and when she is killed it falls into the hands of the narrator of the next novel, a young halberdier.

STRUCTURE AND FOCUS OF HEEDLESS HOPALONG'S STORY

Heedless Hopalong, like all the other novels in the Simplician cycle, is told in the first person. But it differs from the others in that only two-thirds of it is devoted to the story of the titular hero and its protagonist is not the alleged author. Rather, a scribe named Philarchus Grossus von Tromerheim records verbatim Hopalong's story as he told it.

Grimmelshausen probably had several reasons for choosing Philarchus as narrator. First, Philarchus, who is listed on the title page of *The Runagate Courage* and *Heedless Hopalong* as the author, can explain how he came to write and to publish the two works. Thus he describes how he was taken captive by Courage and her gypsy band and was compelled to write down her story as she dictated it to him. He also tells how Simplicissimus asked him to write down Hopalong's story and even paid him generously to do so.

In addition, the choice of Philarchus as narrator made it possible to show that Courage was deceived in her belief that she had foisted off on Simplicissimus a son who was not his. Moreover, Philarchus as the first-person narrator enhances the verisimilitude of *Heedless Hopalong*. Whereas Simplicissimus is intelligent, sensitive, and capable of writing his memoirs, and while Courage, although morally reprehensible, possesses sufficient wit to have composed her autobiography and sufficient malice to have done so out of spite, Hopalong is not the sort of character who would, or could, sit down and commit to paper, or even dictate, the story of his life. Instead, he is the sort of man who might tell an old friend his life story. By making Philarchus the recorder of Hopalong's tale, Grimmelshausen was able to keep Hopalong's character psychologically consistent.

Finally, Grimmelshausen in *Heedless Hopalong* was able to portray, through eyes other than their own, three major Simplician characters. First, there is Courage, now up in years but still as sinful as ever. Then, there is Hopalong, now a lonely old cripple and, at first, an unreconstructed ne'er-do-well. And, most important of all, there is Simplicissimus, who is not, as some of his critics contend, merely a teller of merry tales meant to amuse, but a mature, serious, and pious man whose goal is the moral improvement of his fellow man, either through his personal influence or through his writings.

The structure of *Heedless Hopalong* is of particular significance, for there are numerous indications that it was intended to be tripartite. Indeed, the number three occurs repeatedly. There are three main characters, as is underscored by the title of Chapter 2, *Conjunctio Saturni, Martis & Mercurii,* referring to the three dissimilar men who meet at the inn in Strasbourg: Philarchus, Simplicissimus, and Hopalong. Three women play an influential role in Philarchus' life: the little chambermaid, who tells him that his application for employment has been rejected; Courage, who employs him and then cheats him; and the little gypsy girl, who tricks him into thinking he has married her. There are also three women in Hopalong's life: Courage, the first wife, and the hurdy-gurdy girl. Hopalong tells of three well-known wastrels (Chapter 11) and notes that he had as a young soldier three nicknames

(Chapter 12). He goes on three sea journeys, fights in three wars, is ill three times, and is wounded three times.

There are some indications that Grimmelshausen may have originally conceived *Heedless Hopalong* to be in three parts of nine chapters each. The first nine chapters present the three main figures and set the scene for Hopalong's narration; the second nine focus on Hopalong's experiences in the Thirty Years' War; and the third nine depict his life from the end of the war until he meets Simplicissimus in the inn. There are, furthermore, some similarities in the content of corresponding chapters in the three parts. For example, the number "three" occurs prominently in Chapters 2, 11, and 20 (respectively, the three main characters, the three wastrels, and the three last attempts by the Protestant side to win a decisive victory over the Imperial forces). Chapters 3, 12, and 21 depict tricks played on someone (respectively, Simplicissimus' unwitting trick on the officer, Hopalong's trick on the peasant, and the trick of Hopalong's wife on her customers by adulterating wine). In Chapters 4, 13, and 22 there are encounters with women (respectively, Philarchus' first meeting with Courage, Hopalong's meeting with her, and Hopalong's wooing of the hurdy-gurdy girl). And in Chapters 5, 14, and 23 characters reach significant points in their careers (respectively, Philarchus as Courage's scribe, Hopalong as a soldier, and Hopalong as a beggar). It is clear, however, that if Grimmelshausen began composing *Heedless Hopalong* with the idea in mind of linking corresponding chapters in the three parts in some way, he did not pursue it consistently, for similarities in Chapters 6-15-24, 7-16-25, 8-17-26, and 9-18-27 are hard to find.

Whereas Grimmelshausen did not construct a uniformly tripartite work, he created for each of his three main characters a consistent, distinctive, and identifiable "voice," which contributes to the characterization of each. For example, in *Heedless Hopalong,* Philarchus is introduced for the first time in the Simplician novels. Although his name appears on the title page of Courage's biography, *The Runagate Courage,* he never speaks in his own behalf. He is content, rather, to transcribe her words faithfully, as he does those of Simplicius and Hopalong in *Heedless Hopalong.* His penchant for convoluted sentences, his preference for a foreign word where a good German one would do, his love for rhetorical flourishes, and his predilection for recondite allusions which exhibit the erudition of which he is obviously so proud, all mark him as a callow but pretentious youth who feels he must demonstrate that he is both a scholar and a gentleman. Yet, the impression he leaves is not that which he intends. He is bland, obtuse, and not infrequently confused. His posturing and pedantry are at times ridiculous. Only his tender years mitigate the sophomoric attitude conveyed by his words.

The voice in which Simplicissimus speaks is strikingly different. He can, of course, hold his own with Philarchus when the latter begins to flaunt his book-learning. But Simplicissimus' voice and language are essentially those of a man who recognizes his obligation to save any soul he sees to be in danger of perdition. He speaks the sober, unaffected language of the serious preacher-educator, the *Volksprediger*. Even when he recounts an anecdote like the Simplicissimus of old, he does so only to teach a moral lesson. He can, of course, be witty, mundane, even earthy on occasion. But everything he says is tempered by reason and by the wisdom which he has acquired after years of exposure to life's vicissitudes. His is the kind but stern voice of the father, the teacher, the concerned friend, the upright and responsible Christian.

The third voice, that of Hopalong, is distinct from the other two. From Simplicissimus' point of view, Hopalong's is the voice of unreason. It is an intensely human voice, nonetheless. He is heard among friends, at ease, bantering and arguing back and forth with Simplicissimus, and telling of his hard times in language refreshingly direct, forthright, and lively. He is cynical, irreverent, sarcastic, and coarse. He is also candid, tolerant, and pithy. In Hopalong's mouth, Simplicissimus' long and eloquent sermon on the moral lessons contained in the Magic Book is reduced to a few simple, pointed—and effective—sentences.

The contrasts in character which are implied by the three voices are developed in the actions of Philarchus, Hopalong, and Simplicius. Philarchus' immaturity can be seen by the ease with which he is persuaded by Courage and her gypsies to stray from the path of virtue. His romanticism is evident in his unjustified daydreams when the little chambermaid approaches him. His timidity is revealed by his reaction when Hopalong threatens to physically attack him. He is clearly as pretentious as his name, Philarchus Grossus von Tromerheim.

Hopalong's name derives from the first command Courage gave him—"Hop along and catch our piebald! The cornet here would like to ride him and bargain for him in cash." And his name reveals much about his character. In German, the name, *Spring-ins-feld*, literally means "hop in the field" and is applied to a lively, happy child and, generally in a disparaging way, to a heedless, unbridled youth. The name is apt, for Hopalong has thoughtlessly hopped through life like a child, and is, at the time when he recounts the events of his life, an old beggar hopping along on one leg. By his own account he is not an admirable character. When we meet him, he has little to recommend him other than that at the moment he does not have lice. While he may once have been happy-go-lucky, devil-may-care, one who would make an excellent comrade-in-arms, the only vestiges of the carefree character of his youth are the shopworn tricks with which he attempts to attract an audience. His bravery of earlier years has turned to malice and irascibility, his mischievous humor to guile and craftiness, his carefree lustiness to selfishness. If there is anything appealing in this hard wreck of a man, it is the glimpses of what he once was as he recounts his life and is slowly softened by the stern but kind concern of his old comrade-in-arms Simplicius Simplicissimus. Gradually the picture emerges of an unreflecting man who comes to grips with every new adventure but rarely tries to influence events. The only trade he knows up to his forty-fifth year, aside from juggler's tricks, is soldiering; his only skills fighting and plundering. He boasts to Simplicissimus' old mother that he has stolen so many cattle in his day "that if all of them were tied together tail to horn they would surely reach from here to your farm despite the fact that your farm, I hear tell, is four Swiss miles from here."

Hopalong's actions were no different from those of most other common soldiers during the Thirty Years' War. Since armies lived off the land they had conquered, the greater part of a soldier's time was spent not in fighting, or even in drill, but in search of food for himself and for his unit. A successful soldier was one who had at least one groom or servant who cared for his horses and gear and supported him in battle, as well as a boy who did all the menial chores and looked to the provisions (that is, stole food). Booty, whether money, arms, horses, or provisions, was the primary concern of every soldier, groom, and page. In short, every common soldier was out to take for himself, by force if necessary, anything he could get. It is the application of this wartime ethic to life during peacetime which causes Hopalong to fail ultimately as an innkeeper.

With all these faults, Hopalong has outstanding virtues, too: he is tough, he can endure, he can rebound from any misfortune. But even these assets are the products of his inability or unwillingness to reflect, to think seriously about life and death. When he does philosophize, he only mouths banalities he has heard. Experience has taught him some things, but he fails to draw from his experiences any but the most mundane conclusions. Until he meets Simplicissimus again, he apparently has only once in his life—while trapped by wolves atop a house—reflected on the danger of a life of sin to his immortal soul.

The character of Simplicissimus is opposite to that of both Philarchus and Hopalong. Simplicissimus possesses the intelligence, education, and good breeding to which Philarchus vainly pretends. Unlike Hopalong, Simplicius does reflect; he has thought about the meaning of life and of the Christian ethic. Even though he, like Hopalong, has been a soldier, has known fortune and misfortune, and has been ensnared by sin, he has developed into a man quite different from Hopalong. Therefore, the argument between Simplicissimus and Hopalong, as the Christian rationalist Grimmelshausen probably viewed it, is the argument between reason and unreason, between wisdom and folly. By using Hopalong and Philarchus as foils for Simplicissimus, Grimmelshausen emphasizes that reason and wisdom are more than knowledge garnered by experience and by erudition acquired from books. Both Hopalong and Philarchus have acquired knowledge, Hopalong by experience and Philarchus by study, but Philarchus' erudition does not save him from falling under the evil spell of Courage, nor does Hopalong's experience with Courage protect him from the dubious charms of the hurdy-gurdy girl. It is Grimmelshausen's conviction (and that of serious Christians of his time) that the ability to profit from experience and learning is given to a man by the power of reason which derives from God, the God of *ordo et ratio*. Simplicissimus is such a man, Hopalong is not, and Philarchus is not yet but may one day be.

Grimmelshausen reinforces the characters of the three protagonists of *Heedless Hopalong* by introducing two women who contrast with each other and who point up the differences in the characters of Simplicissimus, Philarchus, and Hopalong. The first woman is Courage, who is seen not through her own eyes or those of Simplicissimus but by an "impartial observer," Philarchus. Courage, who is linked to all three protagonists, is seen in bold relief to both Simplicissimus and

Hopalong. Whereas Simplicius Simplicissimus has seen the danger of a sinful life and renounced it, and Hopalong ultimately comes to realize that his immortal soul is in danger and reforms, Courage has rejected all pleas that she mend her ways. She continues to "wallow in sin" with no thought of repentance. Philarchus' description of her agrees with her autobiographical self-portrait; he likens her to the Whore of Babylon. And she has indeed yielded to her baser instincts until she has become a malevolent and depraved woman. If Simplicissimus is intended to represent the Christian man who finds his way to God through trials and temptation, then Courage represents the woman who, deprived of the guidance of a father, husband, or priest, falls prey to all that is evil in human nature.

The other female figure is the hurdy-gurdy girl, the amoral and uneducated offspring of an arch-beggar. She is not a whit less evil than Courage, but whereas Courage, like Simplicissimus, is drawn on a grand scale, the hurdy-gurdy girl, like Hopalong, is one of the common folk. Courage is a devil. The hurdy-gurdy girl is a poltergeist, a mischievous hobgoblin. The tricks she plays on the townspeople, on the wedding guests, and on the abbess are naive to the point of innocence in their childish lack of inventiveness.

The reactions of the hurdy-gurdy girl and Hopalong to the magic bird's nest are significant. Because she is devoid of morality and has no fear of evil, she is willing to exploit the invisibility which the bird's nest can make possible. Hopalong, by contrast, has sufficient moral instincts to recognize the nest's potential for evil and to renounce the use of it. Without this glimmer of Christian morality, Hopalong would have resisted efforts to convince him to mend his ways, as did both Courage and the hurdy-gurdy girl.

To the reader of Grimmelshausen's time, the reasons for Simplicissimus' superiority to all the other major characters in *Heedless Hopalong* were obvious. In the seventeenth century the two factors which determined whether one would ultimately be a success or a failure as a Christian and as a human being were genealogy and moral education. Simplicissimus has clear advantages in regard to both. First, he is of noble parentage: both his mother and his father are aristocrats and Christians, united in holy matrimony. Second, although his mother dies immediately after his birth and he is at first reared by peasants, he is cared for and given a Christian upbringing by his real father during his formative years. Neither he nor his father knows at that time of their blood relationship, yet Simplicissimus' father, living as a hermit, fulfills his duty toward his son, as a Christian parent should, by providing for his physical needs and safety and by instructing him in the Christian faith.

Philarchus, it is clear, can never become the full equal of Simplicissimus. While Philarchus has presumably had a sound moral upbringing, he is the child of burghers, not of the nobility. In addition he is a coward, devoid of noble instincts, and at best a confused dreamer.

Hopalong, of course, enjoys none of Simplicissimus' advantages. While Hopalong's mother, he tells us, was of patrician stock, she married and ran away with a wandering juggler, a man who, though physically handsome, was little more than a vagabond and mountebank. Moreover, poor Hopalong does not even have the advantage of an upbringing by this ill-matched pair. When Hopalong is still an infant, his real father dies, and another juggler, who marries his mother and takes over his education, is interested only in acquiring wealth by exploiting the talents of his offspring if necessary.

The hurdy-gurdy girl's breeding and moral education are not any better than Hopalong's, in fact they are worse. The beggar's creed, according to which she is reared and which is evident in the contract which her father forces Hopalong to sign, is devoid of morality and based merely on self-interest.

Only Courage, whose parents are of the nobility, has a potential approximating that of Simplicissimus. But Courage is, first of all, an illegitimate child, which, in the eyes of the seventeenth-century reader, would have reduced her potential for success as a Christian and a human being. And, more importantly, she is deprived of a Christian education. Her parents lodge her with a nurse and apparently see that her physical needs are met, at least until the war breaks out, but they do nothing to see that she is instructed in the principles of Christianity. Furthermore, the others in her life who should have undertaken to educate her properly (and the reader in the seventeenth century would have put all her husbands and lovers, including Simplicissimus and Hopalong, into this category) do nothing but exploit her. By the time the clergy, who should also have been responsible for her, begin to urge her to repent and mend her sinful ways, it is too late.

For Courage, as for Simplicissimus and Hopalong, the opportunities for a proper Christian upbringing are indeed slight. All three are separated from their parents at an early age. More importantly, all three grow to maturity under the most adverse circumstances conceivable. The world which confronts them is without order, decency, humanity, and Christian morality. It is a world at war.

THE WARS OF THE SEVENTEENTH CENTURY: HOPALONG'S ROLE

Heedless Hopalong, like *Simplicissimus* and *The Runagate Courage*, describes the life of a participant in the Thirty Years' War. But Hopalong, unlike the other Simplician figures, experiences the whole of that war, and two others as well, as a member of various armies.

The Thirty Years' War began in 1618 with the rebellion of the Bohemian Protestants, who feared that the heir apparent to the Bohemian throne, Archduke Ferdinand of Styria, would institute the Counter-Reformation by force in their land as he had in his own duchy. The rebellion quickly became a full-scale war between Catholic and Protestant lands in Western Europe. Even before the war began, the Spanish Habsburg army, which Hopalong joined as a page to an officer, had been waiting in Flanders for an opportunity to subjugate the Protestant United Provinces of the Netherlands, and while the Austrian and Bavarian Catholic armies were retaking Bohemia from the rebels, part of the Spanish army, and with it Hopalong, invaded the Palatinate, which was of strategic importance because it was the only Protestant territory on the Spanish route of march from Flanders to Italy.

As soon as Bohemia was again in Imperial hands, the Bavarian army, led by Tilly, marched to the Palatinate where it joined forces with the Spanish army and in May 1622 helped defeat the Protestants in the battle of Wimpfen, in which Hopalong, now a drummer boy, fought so bravely that he was allowed to become a musketeer. The two Catholic armies then defeated Prince Christian of Brunswick's newly-raised Protestant army in the battle of Höchst, and the main body of the Spanish army invaded the United Provinces. The Catholics seemed to have won the war when, in 1623, Tilly marched all the way to the Dutch border, but Cardinal Richelieu, Louis XIII's minister of state, organized an alliance between France and the four major Protestant powers—the United Provinces, England, Denmark, and Sweden. The allies' plan to cut the supply lines between Spain and the Habsburg forces in the north failed, however, when in 1626 the Austrian Imperials under Wallenstein, together with Tilly's Bavarians (with whom Hopalong was now serving), defeated the Danish army at Lutter and pursued its remnants down the Elbe, occupying Holstein, Jutland and Magdeburg. During this occupation Hopalong met Courage, bought his release from the army, and became a sutler. When the anti-Habsburg forces, in another attempt to cut Catholic supply lines, occupied the Duchy of Mantua, Emperor Ferdinand reacted by sending an Imperial army, to which Courage and Hopalong were attached, to Italy to reconquer the Mantuan strongholds. The campaign ended with the capitulation of the fortresses in Mantua, and France withdrew from the war. Hopalong, having broken with Courage, now returned to the war as a soldier in the Imperial army.

In 1630, just as the Catholic side seemed to have achieved its objective, fortune turned against it. Gustav Adolph, King of Sweden, invaded Germany with a well-trained Protestant army, and there was no one to face him but Tilly, now old and infirm, and Pappenheim, as rash as he was valorous. In September 1631 the Swedes defeated Tilly and Pappenheim at Breitenfeld and marched westward through Saxony and Hesse to the Rhine, where they captured Hopalong and forced him to serve with them. The Swedes then moved northward along the Rhine as far as Bacharach, where Hopalong was recaptured by the Imperials and impressed into service in Pappenheim's army.

By the end of 1631 the Swedes held much of the Rhineland, most of the northern territories, and were preparing to invade Bavaria. While Pappenheim's Bavarian army, in which Hopalong was serving as a freebooter, was fighting against the Swedes and Hessians in Westphalia, the Imperial army, now commanded by Wallenstein, occupied Prague and suddenly marched toward Saxony, apparently to cut off Gustav Adolph from his northern bases. When Gustav Adolph responded by moving his army westward, Wallenstein called on Pappenheim to join him, and on November 16, 1632, their combined armies engaged the Protestant force commanded by Gustav Adolph in the battle of Lützen, which Hopalong describes in some detail. After long and bitter fighting the Protestants were victorious, but Gustav Adolph was killed, and Pappenheim was mortally wounded. Without their king the

Swedes ceased to be a dominant factor in the war, and without Pappenheim the morale of the Imperials began to slip.

In 1634 it appeared that the Imperials might nevertheless succeed in retaking Germany. The army of King Ferdinand of Hungary and Bohemia retook Regensburg and Donauwörth and laid siege to the fortress of Nördlingen. Augmented by a Spanish army, the Imperials then defeated the Protestants in the battle of Nördlingen and moved northward into Württemberg, Hesse, and Westphalia. Hopalong, who had been put back into his original regiment as a dragoon, participated in Ferdinand's successful campaign as a soldier under the command of Jean de Werdt and, later, of Götz.

Alarmed by the Imperial victories, France re-entered the war, and by 1637 the anti-Habsburg forces were again on the offensive. They reconquered Westphalia, where Hopalong was captured and became a musketeer in the Protestant army; and they swept southward along the Rhine and into Franconia and Württemberg. From 1640 on, the fortunes of the Habsburgs grew steadily worse. The final turning point came in 1643 when Protestant forces destroyed the Spanish infantry in the battle of Rocroi on the Flemish border, thus finally breaking the Spanish Habsburg hold on the United Provinces. Hopalong was once more recaptured by Catholic troops and put back into the regiment of dragoons in which he had originally served. The Bavarian armies now tried desperately to maintain control over the Black Forest and the Danube and thus protect Bavaria from invasion, but they were now fighting for a lost cause. By the spring of 1647 Archduke Maximilian of Bavaria saw no option but to sue for peace, and in March he signed a truce, a "half-way peace," as Hopalong calls it. By September Maximilian was compelled by rapidly changing political conditions to renew alliance with the Emperor, but before the combined Bavarian and Imperial armies could prepare themselves for a last-ditch defense along the Danube, the enemy fell upon them on May 17, 1648, at the village of Zusmarshausen, and put them to rout. The *coup de grace* occurred when Duc d'Enghien trapped the Spanish army of the Netherlands at Lens and completely destroyed it. With Protestant forces in control of the Kleinseite of Prague and about to take the rest of the city, with all of Bavaria and the Rhineland except for a few fortresses (such as the one in which Hopalong was garrisoned) overrun by Protestant armies and exposed to unparalleled pillage and rape, the Emperor and his ally Maximilian of

Bavaria had no recourse but to sign a peace treaty. After thirty years the war was finally over.

While most of Grimmelshausen's readers had probably forgotten the events and horrors of the Thirty Years' War or were too young to remember them, nearly all of them were doubtless familiar with the two other wars in which Hopalong fought. Both conflicts were with the Turks, who were to continue to pose a serious threat to Europe until they were decisively defeated in 1717 by an Austrian army commanded by Prince Eugene. The first such war in which Hopalong participated began in 1663, when Emperor Leopold sent 10,000 men into Transylvania in support of a revolt led by John Keményi, and the Turks responded by sending an army of 120,000 to conquer all of Hungary. Fearing that Vienna would fall to the Ottoman Empire, the German states, both Protestant and Catholic, sent both men and money to help Austria in its struggle, and France contributed 4,000 soldiers to her erstwhile foe (Hopalong went with one such group of volunteers). The Turks were defeated on August 1, 1664, when they attempted to cross the River Raba at St. Gotthard one unit at a time.

The last war in which Hopalong fought had ended only a year or so before his story appeared in print. In 1645 the Turks had landed a large army on the island of Crete, which was under Venetian administration, and in 1648 they began the siege of the fortress of Candia, the capital of Crete. As in the Hungarian-Turkish war, the nations of Europe supplied men and money to continue the struggle against the besieging Turks, but in September 1669, only a short time after Hopalong arrived there, Candia was finally forced to surrender.

Of the three wars in which Hopalong fights, the last one has the most serious physical consequences for him. After more than thirty years of soldiering, he is so seriously wounded that he loses a leg. But psychologically the Thirty Years' War is far more important for him, as it also is for Simplicissimus. Each enters the war a naive and callow youth and emerges from it a mature person. Each experiences extremes in good and bad fortune. Each learns how abruptly one's position in the world can change. Nowhere is the difference between Simplicissimus and Hopalong more clearly portrayed than in their reactions to war. While Simplicissimus recognizes it to be the clearest manifestation of the evil which ever lurks behind the attractive but sinful world, Hopalong regards it as the natural human condition and finds in it, as in the peacetime life of such social outcasts as jugglers and beggars, a congenial way of life, one to which he can return whenever life in ordered society becomes impossible.

CONCLUSION

In *The Singular Life Story of Heedless Hopalong* Grimmelshausen's contemporaries doubtless saw their own *Weltanschauung* reflected and confirmed: that the world is seductive, a testing ground for mankind, and that wise people will ever keep their eyes fixed on the true and eternal treasures of salvation. They were therefore probably as interested in Simplicissimus as in Hopalong, because this world-view is exactly what Simplicissimus is finally able to teach his old but still heedless comrade-in-arms. Today's reader, however, may well feel that Simplicissimus is too high-minded in his persistent efforts to save the soul of his reprobate friend and lacks the vitality and earthy humor which made him such an enchanting figure in his own life story. Because of Hopalong's crudeness, worldliness, and crafty opportunism, he may seem to the modern reader the more vivid and intriguing character.

Grimmelshausen was perturbed, as he remarked in *The Satirical Pilgrim,* that since the end of the Thirty Years' War, a generation had grown up "which would like to see a war for the simple reason that they do not know what war is." *The Singular Life Story of Heedless Hopalong* was probably meant to be a warning to youngsters like Philarchus or Simplicissimus' own son, who hear about war from Hopalong. But in setting out to demonstrate that "if you go a-soldiering when you're young, you'll go begging when you're old," Grimmelshausen created, perhaps unintentionally, one of German literature's finest portraits of the common soldier who does the fighting and suffering and dying. As Hopalong recounts the story of his life, a picture of a soldier emerges which could well be that of any fighting man in any century. They all share Hopalong's traits: his brutality, his dislike for "civilians," his loyalty to his comrades-in-arms, his lack of interest in the political situation responsible for his fate, his admiration for competent commanding officers and his contempt for incompetent ones, his pride in having fought well, his ability to take physical punishment, and his will to survive.

Grimmelshausen's pacifism is attractive. But it is hard not to sympathize with the plight of his common soldier, Hopalong. Like the fighting men portrayed in nearly all war novels, he is tested. His testing ground is a world gone mad, a world in which moral order and civilized values have all but disappeared and men have become little more than beasts trying to survive any way they can. He suffers losses to his body and soul and psyche which he cannot and does not want to assess. And yet his story conveys, as does every good war novel, the conviction expressed by William Faulkner that "man will not merely endure: he will prevail."

Foreign Words and Phrases Used in the Text

agnus dei: Lamb of God (medallion)
armistitium: armistice
battaglia: battle
bestia: beast
cavalcada: body of troops
contagio: contagious disease
copei: semblance
corpo: army
electuarium: electuary, medicine in paste form
exercitia: tricks, physical exercise
faeces: sediment
fatum: fate
harmonia: melody played by two or more instruments
histori, historia: story, history
in litteris: in the study of letters
in summa: to sum up
in summa summarum: to sum up once and for all
Italia: Italy
insationabilis: insatiable
judicium: intelligence, good judgment
lansquenet: mercenary footsoldier, *Landsknecht*
ma foi: by my faith!
materi, materia(m): material, matter, substance
monsieur: gentleman
mores: good manners
niemesy, niemey: a German
officia: positions, posts

oleum populeum: oil of poplar (tree)
pater noster: the Lord's Prayer
patrimonium: patrimony
per accord: through negotiation
per Graeciam: through Greece
pistor: baker
praeceptor(ibus): teacher(s)
principia: principles
pryc: finished
recta: directly
reputatio: reputation
salva guardi: garrison duty
secretarius: secretary
serviteur: lover
Sicilia: Sicily
Sol . . . Luna: Sun . . . Moon
soldateska: soldiers
spectra: ghosts, spirits, phantoms
studiosi: students
summa: sum, amount
theriac: patent medicine, nostrum, cure-all
tirones: recruits
valet(s)-de-chambre: manservant(s)
viaticum: money to help defray travel expenses
victoria: victory
vocativus: rogue, scamp

THE BALLAD OF HOPALONG

They called me madcap Hopalong,
    Those many years ago,
When I was young and brash and proud
    And longed to fight the foe,
To fight for glory, wealth, and fame
    Until my dying breath,
And, if Fortuna frowned on me,
    To die a soldier's death.
And how did I fare at the hands of fate?
    And what did Fortune decree?
They conspired to show how fickle they are,
    For they sure mistreated me.

I became a toy in Fortune's hands
    And went where I was led,
Until she took my leg from me
    And gave me a peg instead.
Now I'm obliged to hobble about
    And beg from door to door
For a crust of bread from the very folk
    I robbed of their bread in the war.
Let my wretched life be a warning to you
    To whom this tale is told:
If you go a-soldiering when you're young,
    You'll go begging when you're old.

THE SINGULAR LIFE STORY OF HEEDLESS HOPALONG

That is,
an amusing, merry and right droll
biography of a once fresh, brave, tried
and true soldier, now, however,
a haggard, worn-out, but still right
sly runagate and beggar.
Together with his wondrous MAGIC BOOK.

Composed and writ down, at the behest of
the widely known and world famous Simplicissimi,
by Philarcho Grosso von Tromerheim

PRINTED IN PAPHLAGONIA
BY FELIX STRATIOT
ANNO 1670

CHAPTER 1

For what galling reason the Author was moved to compose this little book

This past Christmas fair,[1] when I was waiting with most peevish patience in the courtyard of a noble lord to receive a reply to a petition in which I had requested very movingly a position as a clerk and in which I had boasted in most pious words of my great diligence, also affirming in sufficient measure the steadfastness of my incomparable loyalty, and when the desired response was simply not forthcoming, look you, I became all the more impatient; particularly since I saw that dirty scullery and stinking stable rabble were allowed to pass in and out, while I, on the other hand, was being treated with contempt, like an unsalted codfish no longer worth tasting. At that time I entertained all kinds of ideas and crotchets, and it seemed to me that I could read in the sneering faces of the aforementioned fellows that they might eventually presume to chaff me and make sport of me if I either did not soon receive a favorable reply, or else did not depart of my own accord without one. But then my thoughts took another turn, and I reassured myself of a far better outcome. "Patience! patience!" said I to myself. "Day was not built in a Rome" (for my words came out topsy-turvy, because I was all confused). "If you obtain this position, you can make these carrion dogs pay for their contemptuance."[2] However, I was not only plagued by these fellows and by daily inner doubts, but also outwardly by the then prevailing bitter cold,[3] in such manner that anyone who saw me and did not himself feel the cold would have sworn a thousand oaths that I was afflicted with three- or four-day ague. The servants ran hither and thither, paying little attention nor speaking to me. At the very moment when I was feeding and nourishing myself best with high hopes, I espied a lovely little chambermaid, to whom I straightway lost my heart, for when she walked *recta* towards me I could not but imagine that this was an indubitable omen that I should become her *serviteur*. My heart jumped for joy, as it were, because my folly assured me such great, future happiness. But when she came up to me and opened her

1

cherry-red little mouth, she said: "My dear fellow, what is your business here? Are you perchance a poor scholar who is perhaps desirous of alms?" Thereupon I straightway thought to myself: "These words have destroyed all your hopes!" For because we clerks have and possess just as arrogant minds—why do I say "arrogant"?—I meant to say "lofty" minds—as for instance even tailors, who inveigle themselves into the good graces of great lords and masters by first becoming their *valets-de-chambre*, and finally their lords and masters (just think how confused I was at that moment, since even now I am stating everything in such an erroneous and confused manner)—what I meant to say was "by first becoming *valets-de-chambre*, and finally their *own* lords and masters" (because great lords will hardly set either clerks or tailors above themselves as their lords and masters). And so it seemed to me that the maid should have accommodated herself to what I was imagining and should have said to me: "What business does the honorable gentleman desire to pursue here?" Well, why waste words on this? I was completely dismayed, and yet I was unable to accuse the maid of any effrontery, since she had posed her question very properly. Moreover, I could scarcely find in my *Capitolio*[4] (as the old Romans called their armory) sufficient words from the stores of them which I had in it to counter properly this first blow, which seemed to me more painful than a sharp box on the ears. But finally, with my voice trembling and quaking from fear, hope, and cold, I did stammer out this much: that I was that *monsieur* who, upon the recommendation of honorable folk, hoped to become her master's clerk. "Oh, my dear God!" answered this young crowbait. "Are you that one? Alas, put such thoughts out of your mind, for anyone desirous of that position which you aspire to must either pay my gracious lord one thousand sovereigns as bond, or else find someone to vouch for him in that amount. Three days ago I was given half a sovereign to give to you whenever you might report, but our naughty servants did not even tell me that you were here, else I should not have let you stand about this long in this cold." You can well imagine the look on my face when I heard this. I thought to myself: "Let Venus lay on, and Vulcan will have need of one less servant!"[5] I was quite unwilling to accept the proffered half-sovereign, for which reason I resisted, because I thought that such a dismissal would be contrary to, and disgraceful to, my clerkly *reputatio*. But then I thought to myself: "Who knows when and where this lord may not be able to do you a favor in the future?'' for which reason I stuffed it into my pocket and took hope that with time and patience I still might obtain the desired position, a chance which I should forfeit, along with the lord's good graces, should I so stubbornly and disdainfully refuse to accept this pittance.

Thus I accepted my dismissal, and the maid herself accompanied me as far as the gate, because she wanted to lock it straightway because of the approaching noonday meal. There we were, presenting each other our compliments in regard to, as well as because of, the half-sovereign, when the maid let slip these words: "Just go ahead and take it, and let me assure you that my gracious lord and his lady do not let even the slightest service go unrewarded, be it only lighting their way to the privy.'' That vexed me so sorely and so got my dander up that I answered the maid, more impudently than prudently. "Then tell your gracious lord,'' I said, "that if he intended to pay me as much for each sheet of paper which he uses to wipe his noble arse, for which purpose he may have unwisely used my petition before reading it, he'd sooner lack money than I the paper, quills or ink.'' Thereupon I trundled up the long street, not because I wished to, but because in my anger I did not care where I went. I felt so ungrateful towards those who had led me astray *in litteris* that I even regretted that I had not told my *praeceptoribus* to kiss my arse when they occasionally made me bare it to chastise me. "Alas!'' I said. "Why ever did not your parents have you learn a trade, or how to thresh, or cut thatch, or something like that? Then, after all, you would find work now with any peasant and would not be obliged to cool your heels in the presence of great lords in order to flatter them. If only you were skilled in the most menial trade imaginable, you would find masters who would take you in for the sake of said trade and give you the customary *viaticum*, even though they did not give you any work, etc. But in your profession, not a soul cares about you, and you are the most contemptible sluggard alive!'' Exasperated as I was, I walked a long way, but the more my ire abated, as it did by and by, the more I felt the cruel cold, to which hitherto I had paid scant attention. Yes, it so tormented me that I sighed for a warm room, and inasmuch as an inn happened to be straight ahead of me, I went inside, more for the sake of the warmth than to quench my thirst.

CHAPTER 2

Conjunctio Saturni, Martis, & Mercurii[1]

There I was received much more courteously than I had been by the aforementioned curt chambermaid, for the manservant came straightway and asked: "What does the gentleman wish to have?" Although I had spent all day thinking about a clerk's position, but was now thinking about the stove's warmth, I nevertheless said to him: "A good half-measure of wine," which in fact he straightway served me, for the place was not a bathhouse, where one pays for the heat, but a place for food where the necessary warmth is free, or at least is reckoned into the bill.

I sat down with my half-measure of wine very near to the stove so as to warm myself properly. At the very same table sat a man who was eating *à la carte,* and he was eating like a horse, and falling to so mightily, with both cheeks full, that I marveled at him. He had already put away a bowl of soup and had then gobbled down two portions of cabbage and meat when I arrived, and now, in addition, he was asking for a large piece of roast, which request caused me to observe him more closely. Then I saw that not merely in regard to eating, but also in physical appearance, he was much different from any man I had ever before seen in my life, for in regard to bodily proportions he was as large as if he had been born in Chile or Chica.[2] His beard was as long and as broad as the innkeeper's slate, on which he notes what the guests have been served. The hair on his head, however, seemed to me like that which up till then I had imagined *Nabuchodonosor*[3] might have worn during his exile. He was wearing a black woolen smock which went down to his knees and was lined, edged, and backed at the seams with green woolen cloth, so that it looked quite strange and almost like a toga of classical antiquity. Next to him lay his long pilgrim's staff, with two knobs at the top, and at the bottom fitted with a long iron point so thick and strong that with one stroke one might easily have administered extreme unction with it.

I was sheer smitten with folly at the sight of this strange attire, and the longer I looked at him, the more I became aware that in growth and

4

color his enormous beard flew in the face of all reason, that is, it was unlike any European beard, for the hair which had grown only nigh on to half a year was dun-colored, while the older hair was pitch black, whereas in others' beards of like color the hair closest to the skin is black, and the older the rest is, the more dun-colored or weather-beaten it usually looks. I cogitated about the cause of this and could think of no other but that the black hair must have grown in a hot country and the dun-colored in a much colder one, and this indeed was the case, for when this man was obliged to wait for his roast and to pause a moment in his eating, he set to drinking, whereupon he could do no less than toast me if he wished that anyone bless his own drink for him, for other than myself there was no other guest there. And since my mouth, which the cruel cold had quite benumbed and frozen shut, had now begun to thaw out a bit, look you, we fell into a conversation with each other, in which I asked first of all whether he had not returned from India only approximately a half a year ago, but so that he might not have cause to answer "What business is that of yours?" I phrased my speculation, to my way of thinking, quite politely, for I said: "Would the most honorable gentleman be so kind as to forgive an impertinent youth, should he make so bold as to ask whether the gentleman did not return from India only a half a year ago?" He was surprised, looked at me, and replied: "If you have otherwise no information or knowledge concerning my person, but are rather now seeing me for the first time, then I ascribe to your youth not impertinence but a sound mind and the same sort of *judicium,* which aroused in you a desire to know for certain what your mind grasped and your *judicium* reasoned out about me. Therefore, tell me first from what you deduced that a half a year ago I was still in India, after which I shall give you to understand whether you judged correctly concerning myself and my journey." Now when I told him that it was the hair of his beard which caused me to understand this, he replied that I was correct and that this proved at the same time that there was more to me than met the eye.

Hereupon he urged me to join him in drinking. But I was reluctant because he mixed his wine. He had drawn from his pocket a tin box in which there was an *electuarium* which looked in every way like theriac.[4] From that same *materi* he took as much as covers the point of a knife and mixed it with the new wine in a small common drinking glass (for he was not drinking aged wine, but only new two-penny wine);

from this, the wine turned so thick and yellow that it sheer resembled a disgusting *purgation,* or at least old olive oil. Now each time when he was about to drink, he poured a single drop of it into the glass, whereupon the milky colored new wine forthwith changed in color, in that all of the unfermented *faeces*[5] in it settled to the bottom and it took on the color of gold, like a wine long laid down. He saw very well that I had no particular desire for his drink and therefore said that I should drink heartily, it would not harm me, and when he persuaded me to try the wine, I found it to be so lovely, hearty, and good that I should have taken it for Malvoisier or Spanish wine if I had not seen that it was only a green Alsatian one. Then he told me that he had learned this art from the Armenians, and demonstrated by his work that an old wine, long laid down and of itself quite delicious, such as I then had before me, was not improved as much by far by this *elixir,* as he called it, as a common green wine was. The reason which he gave for this was that the green wine still had all its strength and had not yet lost any of it, as happens to old wine after a few years.

Now, as we were conversing about the wine and this art of his, there entered the room an old beggar with a pegleg who, like me, had been driven by the cold to the stove in the room. He had hardly warmed himself a bit when he drew forth a small treble violin, tuned it, stepped up to our table, and played a tune. At the same time he so artfully hummed and squeaked with his lips that anyone who only heard him but did not see him would have perforce believed that three different stringed instruments were being played. He was rather poorly clad for the winter, and to all appearances had not had a good summer either, for his haggard body bore witness that he had been obliged to tighten his belt, and his sparse hair that he also must have suffered through a serious illness. Black Smock, who was sitting with me, said to him: "Neighbor, where did you lose your leg?"

"In Candia,[6] sir," the man replied.

Whereupon the other man said: "That is too bad."

"Oh no, not so bad at all," answered Pegleg, "for now I feel the cold in only one leg, and besides I need only one shoe and one stocking."

"Tell me," Black Smock went on, "are you not Hopalong?"

"In times gone by I was," answered the man. "But now I'm Limpabout, for as the old proverb says, 'If you go a-soldiering when you're young, you'll go begging when you're old.' But how did the gentleman recognize me?''

''By your artful music,'' answered the other, ''the likes of which I heard more than thirty years ago in Soest. Did you not at that time have a comrade with the dragoons[7] garrisoned there who called himself Simplicius?''

And when Hopalong acknowledged that this was so, Black Smock said:

''Well I am that same Simplicius.''

At this Hopalong said in surprise: ''The devil take you!''

''What!'' Simplicius said to him. ''Are you not ashamed that you, already an old cripple, are still so crude, godless, and insolent as to greet your old comrade with such words?''

'''Ods hundred sacks o' rents![8] I suppose you're any better!'' said Hopalong, ''or have you perchance turned into a saint since last we met?''

Simplicius answered: ''Even though I am no saint, I have nonetheless surely striven with advancing years to put aside the evil ways of my heedless youth, and am of the opinion that that would be more becoming also to your age than curses and blasphemy.''

''Brother,'' answered Hopalong very respectfully, ''forgive me this time, and let bygones be bygones. I have no desire to dispute with you about anything, unless it be perchance a few tankards of wine.''

And with these words, sitting down quite unbidden, he drew forth an old rag, untying it and saying: ''And so that you may not perchance believe that the beggar Hopalong wishes to sponge off you, well, look you here. I too still have a few pence which are at your service.'' And with that he shook out onto the table a handful of ducats, which I judged to be more than two hundred, and ordered the manservant to bring him a measure of wine also, which, however, Simplicius would not permit, but instead gave him some of his own wine, asking what need there be to put on airs with money, and telling him to put it away because he, Simplicius, had indeed seen more than enough of that himself.

CHAPTER 3

A ridiculous joke which was played
on a drinking companion

I could not but be astonished and happy to be present at this unforeseen meeting of these two men, of whom I had read so many strange things in Simplicissimus' biography, and about whom I myself, at the behest of Courage, had written similar things. When their argument had ended and Simplicius had poured a glass of wine, which he had drunk to Hopalong's health, yet another guest entered whom I took, because of his clothing and his youth, to be such as I, that is, a clerk. He too went to the same spot by the stove where first I and later Hopalong had stood, almost as if all newly arrived guests were first obliged to stand there before they were permitted to sit down. And straightway thereafter a peasant from the other bank of the Rhine followed, who without doubt was a vintner. He doffed his cap before the first man and said: "Steward,[1] sir, I pray ya, give me a sovereign so that I can get me hoes from the blacksmith's where I've had 'em mended."

"What the devil do you mean?" the other answered. "What are you doing taking your hose to the smith? I should think that you would take them to the tailor."

"Me hoes! Me hoes!" said the peasant.

"I hear you!" answered the steward. "Do you think I'm deaf? I am only puzzled about what you're doing with your hose at the blacksmith's when it's a tailor who usually alters or mends hose."

"Ah, Steward, sir," said the peasant, "I am not talkin' of *hose* but of me *hoes,* wherewith I hoe in the vineyard."

"Oh, now I understand," answered the steward. "That's different." And with that he gave the peasant a sovereign, which he also noted down straightway on his writing tablet. I, however, thought to myself: "How can you be a steward over vintners when you don't know anything about hoes?" For the steward ordered the peasant to bring the hoes to him so that he could see just what they were and what the blacksmith had done to them.

Simplicius, however, who had also been listening to this conversation, broke out laughing and laughed till he shook, which in fact was the first and last time I ever saw or heard him laugh, for otherwise he comported himself in a very grave manner, and although he spoke in a rough and manly voice, he was more gracious and amiable than he looked, albeit he was in fact right sparing with words. Hopalong, for his part, demanded to know the cause of this laughter, and did not leave off begging Simplicius till the latter finally said that the steward's misunderstanding of the peasant's words had put him in mind of a comical incident for which he, in his youthful innocence, had been responsible, against his will to be sure, because of a word which he had misunderstood, for which misunderstanding he had nevertheless received a good beating.

"Ah, what was that?" asked Hopalong.

" 'Tis bootless," answered Simplicius, "that I should goad you on to vain folly, which I take immoderate laughter to be, without which, however, you could not hear this *histori,* for I should be burdening my soul by leading another into sin."

I put in my two pence worth and said: "And yet, most honored sir, you yourself included in your biography so many a droll anecdote, why then should you be unwilling now to relate a single comical incident to please your old comrade?"

"That I did," answered Simplicius, "because almost no one wants to look at the naked truth, much less hear it; therefore I dressed up the truth and thereby made it pleasing to men, that they would listen to and accept in good grace what I was intent on correcting here and there in men's manners and morals. And in fact, my friend, you may rest assured that I often feel pangs of conscience for having been too frivolous in that same biography more than once."

I replied in turn, saying: "Laughter is innate to man and not only distinguishes him from all other animals, but is also useful, as we read, for example, that laughing Democritus lived in good health to the age of 109, while weeping Heraclitus,[2] by contrast, died a miserable death at an early age, and, as a matter of fact, in a cow's hide wherein he had had himself sewn in order to heal his limbs; for which reason Seneca,[3] in his *liber de tranquillitate vitae,* where he mentions these two philosophers, admonishes us to follow the example of Democritus rather than that of Heraclitus."

Simplicius answered: "Weeping is in fact just as peculiar to man as is laughter. Nevertheless, to laugh or to weep all the time, as those two men did, would be folly, for there is a proper time for everything. And besides, weeping is more innate to man than laughter, for not only do all men weep when they first come into the world (the sole exception being King *Zoroastris,* who laughed straightway when he was born, although the same is also reported of *Nerone*),[4] but Jesus Christ our Saviour Himself wept on several occasions,[5] but that He ever laughed can nowhere be found in Holy Scripture. On the contrary, He said 'Blessed are those who weep and mourn, for they shall be comforted.'[6] Seneca, being a heathen, may well prefer laughter to tears, but we Christians have greater cause to weep at men's wickedness than to laugh at their folly, for we know that the sins of the laughers will be followed by eternal wailing and lamentation."

" 'Pon my word of honor!" Hopalong then said. "I do believe that you have become a bloody priest!"

"You silly ass!" Simplicius answered him. "How dare you have the gall to swear so frivolous an oath, when your own eyes tell you that it is not true? Do you have any idea at all what it means to swear upon your word of honor?"

Hopalong could not but be a little ashamed and asked forgiveness, for Simplicius' face was so serious and forbidding that it would have frightened anyone.

I, however, said to Simplicius: "Inasmuch as the most honorable gentleman's speeches and writings are full of moral lessons, there can be no doubt that the story which he recalls with such hearty laughter must be both amusing and instructive." And I added the plea that he should tell it without overmuch concern.

"The story," answered Simplicius, "teaches nothing less than that anyone who asks for something he needs should use words and language in such a way that the person he asks can understand them quickly and can make haste to give a correct answer; in addition, it teaches that if one who has been asked a question does not actually, and for sure, understand it, he should politely request the other, particularly if he be of higher rank, to repeat his question. My droll tale is as follows:

"When I was still a page of the Governor of Hanau,[7] he once had as guests some high-ranking officers, among whom were also several from the regiment of the Duke of Weimar,[8] and these he toasted most assiduously. Our officers and the visitors had divided into two camps, as it were, each of which was trying to outdrink the other. The ladies arose and betook themselves to their chambers right after the sweetmeats had been served, because custom forbade that they drink with the men. The gentlemen, however, challenged each other to stand and fill themselves with drink, and several were even leaning against the doors to the room so that none might flee this battle (which reminds me of the torture by which Tiberius, the Roman emperor, killed so many men, for when he wanted to have them executed he first had them forced to drink a lot, and then he had their most worthy urinary tracts tied shut in such a way that they could not pass water, but instead could not but finally die an indescribably painful death).[9] Finally one gentleman did escape, and he had no greater purpose and desire than to pass water, and because his need was doubtless so great, he ran like a dog which has been scalded with hot water runs from a kitchen, in which haste the gentleman, to his misfortune and my own, happened upon me and asked: 'Boy, where is the privy?' At that time I no more knew what a 'privy' was than did German Michel,[10] and I thought he was asking after the 'privy chamber,' as the private apartment of the general and his lady was called, to which place, as I just related, the ladies had betaken themselves. So I pointed out the chamber at the end of the hall and said: 'In there!' Whereupon he ran off toward it like a knight in a tourney who, with leveled lance, rushes to meet the foe. He was so quick that in a single instant he tore open the door, rushed into the room, and let fly with a mighty stream, in full view and presence of the assembled ladies. Now what each party thought and how altogether dismayed each was, you can judge well enough for yourself. I received a beating because I had not pricked up my ears enough; the officer, however, was the butt of mockery because he had not spoken to me in words which I could understand.''

CHAPTER 4

The Author falls in with a band of gypsies and tells of his encounter with Courage

I told Simplicius that it was a pity that he had not also included this story in his biography, but he answered that if he had tried to include all anecdotes of that sort, his book would have been longer than Stumpf's *Swiss Chronicle*.[1] And moreover, he said, he was sorry that he had put in so many ridiculous things because he saw that people were using his book instead of *Till Eulenspiegel's Merry Pranks*, more to while away the time than to learn something worthwhile from it; whereupon he asked me what I myself thought of his book, and whether I had been changed by it for the better or for the worse. I answered that my *judicium* was much too slight either to criticize or to praise it, and even though I had been obliged to write, not against his book, but against him, Simplicissimus, and in so doing had not treated Hopalong over gently either, I nevertheless neither praised nor criticized his book, but instead learned at that time that a person who is outnumbered must comply with the will and demands of those in whose power he happens to be. When I had said this and spoken in my mother tongue, in good Swiss German, which dialect other Germans are wont to regard as crude, if not even arrogant and impolite, Hopalong, who had also been listening and pricking up his ears like an old wolf, when he heard me say his name, said to me in Swiss: "'Ods bodikins! Ya ninny, if ah had ya out o'doors to maself, ah'd bust ya noggin, would ah!"

But Simplicius answered him: "I should well nigh have said, you conceited old ass, that the time has passed when you and I were in Soest and ruled, as it were, over the whole countryside as our whims dictated. With your pegleg you are obliged to dance to a different piper now, or be aware that if you behave too rudely, they will put you in a stone cloak, or even in a Spanish one.[2] In this free city[3] everyone is free to say what he will, but anyone who kicks over the traces must answer for it or bear the consequences."

To me, however, Simplicius posed the question, who or what had compelled me to write against his person, and what particularly surprised him was that along with him I had also been obliged to mention Hopalong too, with whom, after all, he had not spent more than nine months out of his whole life.

I answered: "If the most honorable gentleman, and I don't see any other gentleman hereabouts, may bear with the truth and will pardon me for what I have done, and also protect me from this importunate fellow, Hopalong, about whose humors and frivolity I learned long ago from stories which were dictated to me, then I shall tell both of you such astounding tales about yourselves that you will both be astounded at them; with the assurance, of course, that if I had known the most honorable gentleman to be possessed of such laudable qualities as I now see with my very own eyes, I should, in regard to his person, never have set pen to paper, even though the gypsies had straightway broken my neck."

Now even though Simplicius had a great desire to hear what I should have to say, he nevertheless first said: "My friend, it would be heedless stupidity, indeed contrary to all justice, and evidence of a tyrannical mind, if we were to punish another for things of which we ourselves are guilty. If you have described my vices in your writings, then I shall bear it with patience and equanimity, for I have censured the vices of others thoroughly and in detail (although using pseudonyms, so that I might not besmirch their honor). If it angers those whom I have touched, then why did they not lead more virtuous lives, or why did they give me cause to censure such vices and follies as were unknown to me in my youthful innocence till I had seen them? Go ahead and tell your tale. I shall promise and assure everything you have desired and begged of me."

I answered: "Whether I speak or remain silent, soon all the world will know what I was perforce obliged to write down." Then I turned to Hopalong and asked him whether he had not had in Italy a concubine by the name of Courage. He answered: "That bloody witch! May lightning strike her dead! Is that devil still alive? Since God created the world the sun has never shone on a more wanton *bestia*."

"Now, now," Simplicius said to him, "what manner of wanton heedless talk is this?"

But to me he said: "Pray continue, or rather begin the tale which I so heartily desire to hear."

I answered: "Noble Sir, you will probably soon tire of it, for she is that same woman whom you yourself mentioned in the sixth chapter of the fifth book of your life history."[4]

"No matter," answered Simplicius, "just tell what you know of her, and do not spare my feelings either." Thereupon I told what Simplicius desired to know, in the following manner.

"At the very end of last autumn,[5] when, as everyone knows, there was a delightful Indian summer, I was on my way from my fatherland to the Rhine, to the place where we are now, in fact, where I hoped either to continue my studies while working as a tutor, as is customary with poor students, or to find a post as a clerk, which had been recommended to me by my relatives, from whom I had received letters of introduction for this purpose; now as I was wandering along the crest of the Black Forest on this side of Krummenschiltach, I saw in the distance a sizeable group of ragtag rabble coming towards me whom I at first glance recognized to be gypsies, and I was not mistaken either; and because I did not trust them I hid in the thickest part of a hedge; but these fellows had with them many dogs, both trackers and greyhounds, and they straightway caught my scent, surrounded me, and began to bark as if they had found a piece of game; their masters heard this and hastened up with their guns or long bandoleer muskets to where I was; one posted himself here, another there, just like hunters watching for flushed and driven game. Now when I saw with my own eyes what danger I was in, particularly since the dogs were already beginning to snap at me, I began to cry out as if they had already put the hunting knife to my throat; thereupon everyone—men, women, boys, and girls—ran up, and there was so much ado that I could not tell whether these nasty people meant to kill me or to save me from their dogs. Indeed, in my fright I imagined that they murdered people like me whom they caught in lonely places and afterwards even ate them up so that their murder might go undetected. I wondered too, and I still do, why such infamous gangs of thieves are permitted to rove about the land with their dogs and guns, and I cursed those responsible for the game and hunting rights for tolerating them.

"Now when I found myself surrounded by them this way, like a poor wretch who is about to be hanged and who himself doesn't know whether he be still alive or already half dead, look you, there came riding up on a mule a magnificent gypsy woman, the likes of whom I had never seen or heard of in all my days, for which reason I could not but take her to be at least a distinguished princess, over all the other gypsy women, if not the queen of the gypsies herself! She appeared to be a person of about sixty years, but as I have since reckoned she was one or maybe six years older than that; she did not even have pitch-black hair like the others, but rather it was somewhat yellowish and gathered together with a string of gold and precious stones like a crown, not with a simple band like other gypsy women wear, or with a piece of gauze or a veil or even with just a withe; one could see by her face, which was still smooth, that in her youth she had not been ugly; in her ears she wore earrings fashioned in gold and enamel and studded with diamonds, and around her neck was a string of matched pearls of which a princess need not have been ashamed; her cape was not of rough blanket cloth but of scarlet and was lined with green velvet; both her cape and her skirt, which was of expensive green English cloth, were trimmed with silver lace; she wore neither bodice nor doublet, but did have on a pair of jolly Polish boots; the seams of her shirt were stitched in the Bohemian manner with black silk and it was of pure, snow-white Urach[6] linen, so that all in all she looked like a huckleberry in a bowl of milk; nor did she carry her long gypsy knife hidden under her skirt, but had it in the open, because it was so beautiful that it well deserved to be displayed; and if I am to confess the truth, it still seems to me that the old hag, especially on assback (I very nearly said on horseback), looked extremely good in this costume; and to this very day I can see her this way in my imagination whenever I wish.''

CHAPTER 5

In which Courage dictates her life history to the Author

"Now this preposterous gypsy woman, whom the others all called Milady, but whom I should have taken to be the spitting image of the Lady of Babylon[1] if she had only been astride a seven-headed dragon and had been a bit more beautiful, said to me: 'Ah, my pretty young fair-skinned fellow, what are you doing here all alone and so far from other people?'

"I answered: 'Most noble and powerful lady, my home is in Switzerland, and it is my intention to journey to a city on the Rhine, either to continue my studies there or to go into service, for I am a poor student.'

" 'Well, God keep you, my child,' she said and then she asked, 'Would you not like to serve me with your quill for a day or a fortnight and write somethin' down for me? I would give you a dollar a day.'

"I thought: 'A dollar a day is not to be spurned, but who knows what you will have to write? Such a grand offer must be considered suspect.' And if she herself had not said that God should keep me, I should have thought that she was an apparition of the devil who wished to beguile me with this money and take me into that miserable congregation, the witches' coven. My answer was: 'If it will do me no harm, Milady, I shall write whatever you desire.'

" 'But of course not, my child,' she replied, 'it will not do you any harm at all, God forbid, now come along with us; I shall give you food and drink in the bargain, the best I have, till you have finished the work.'

"Now because I had no more food in my stomach than I had money in my purse, which was empty, and particularly since I was the prisoner of these thieving varmints, look you, I went along with them, namely, into a thick forest where we camped the first night and where several fellows were already at work butchering a handsome stag; now they began lighting fires, cooking and roasting; and as far as I could tell, and afterwards this was completely confirmed, Milady Libushka,[2] for that was the name of my gypsy woman, was in command of everything; a tent of white fustian, which she had under the saddle of her mule, was put up for her. She, however, led me off a little to one side, sat down under a tree, bade me to sit down beside her, and drew forth the life history of Simplicissimus.

" 'Look you, my friend,' she said, 'this knave, about whom this book is written, has played me the scurviest trick[3] that was ever played me in all my living days, which so pains me that I find it impossible to let his knavery go unavenged; for after he had sufficiently enjoyed my gracious good will, this ungrateful rascal (Noble Sir, forgive me for using her own words) saw fit not only to forsake me and to rid himself of me by means of as wicked a trick as was ever heard of, but then even went and proclaimed to the whole world his everlasting disgrace and my own. To be sure, I have already paid him back properly for that first prank he played on me. My chambermaid had been left with an illegitimate child at the very time when this fine fellow was keeping company with me in Sauerbrunnen.[4] When I heard that he had gotten married I had this child baptized in his name and left on his doorstep with a note that I myself had conceived and borne this fruit by him, which caused him to believe that he was obliged to accept and bring up this child as his own, to his own great dishonor; and on top of that he was severely punished by his magistrate; this deceit came off so well that I would not take a thousand sovereigns for it, particularly since I learned to my great joy only recently that this bastard is to be the sole heir of the deceived deceiver.' "

Simplicius, who had been listening attentively, interrupted me at this point and said: "If I still found pleasure in that sort of foolishness, as I once did, it would greatly amuse me to hear that this foolish woman imagines that she pulled the wool over my eyes in this matter, since actually she has done me the greatest service while to this day deceiving herself with vain dreams; for at the time when I was making up to her I lay more often with her chambermaid than with her herself; and it is much more agreeable to me that this same chambermaid and not that wanton gypsy woman is the mother of my son, Simplicius, whom I cannot disown since he takes after me in both mind and body. But here is an example of how those who think to deceive others often deceive themselves and of how God is wont to punish the great sins of those who will not reform with even greater sins, so that their final damnation is that much greater; but pray continue with your tale; what else did she say?''

I obeyed and continued in the following manner: ''She commanded me to acquaint myself a little with your biography, Noble Sir, so that I might use it as a model, for it was her desire that I write down her life story in this very same manner, in order to communicate it likewise to the whole wide world, for the sole purpose of spiting you, Simplicissimus, so that everyone should laugh at your folly; she said I should forget all other thoughts and cares which I might be entertaining at present so that I could attend the better to this work; in the meantime she would secure paper, ink and quill and would pay me, once the work was completed, so that I could not but be satisfied with her.

''So for the first two days I had nothing else to do but to read, to gorge myself with food, and to sleep, during which time, Noble Sir, I finished up your life history; but on the third day, when the writing was to begin, there was an unexpected alarm, not because anyone attacked or pursued us, but because a lone gypsy woman, disguised as a poor beggar, arrived in camp, bringing with her rich booty which she had snatched, such as silverware, rings, medallions, baptismal presents, and all sorts of things which are generally put around children's necks at christenings; at once there was a curious clamor and then a hasty departure. Courage (for that is what this most distinguished gypsy woman called herself in her *Spite-Simplex*) arranged the order of march and divided the whole rabble into various troupes, instructing them which road each troupe was to take and also how, where, and when they should come together again at a certain place which she named. Now when in an instant the entire company had split up like quicksilver and disappeared, Courage herself, together with the ablest and best armed gypsy men and women, rode down into the Black Forest in such great haste as if she herself had stolen the things and were being pursued by a whole army; she did not stop running either till we had put behind us the valleys of Schutt, Kinzig, Peter, Oppenau, Kapp, Sassbach, and Bühl and had reached the large tall forests on the uppermost crest of the Black Forest above the Murg River;[5] there we again set up our camp; a horse had been assigned to me for this rapid journey, and on it I fared as the old saw says: a man who seldom horses doth ride, will feel it betimes . . . etc.[6]

"I well remarked that this retinue of Courage, which counting me consisted only of men and women and thirteen horses, but of no children, carried and safeguarded all the gold, silver, and jewels that the other gypsies had stolen. Nothing astounded me more than the fact that these people knew so well all the paths, all the highways and byways in this wild, desolate region and that with this otherwise disorderly mob everything was so well arranged, and was done in more orderly fashion than in many a household. Scarcely had we eaten that same evening and rested a little when two of the women were clad in the traditional dress of the region and sent to Horb[7] under the pretext of buying bread from a village innkeeper, while at the same time one of the men rode to Gernsbach[8] and brought back the next day a few barrels of wine which, so he told anyone who asked, he had bought from a vintner.

"It was here, Noble Sir, that this godless Courage began to dictate to me her *Spite-Simplex,* as she called it, or better, the story of her wanton life; she did not talk to me in gypsy dialect, but instead in a manner which showed her good intellect and also made it clear that she had lived with gentlefolk and through the wondrous vagaries of fortune had seen the world far and wide, learning and experiencing much. I found her extremely vengeful, and I cannot but believe that Anacharsis himself[9] must have been her teacher, and because of this godless inclination she had the aforementioned treatise written in her own name in order to honor you, Sir. I shall say no more as to the content of this same treatise, since no doubt she will have it printed soon.'"[10]

CHAPTER 6

The Author continues with the aforementioned materia *and tells of the thanks which he received from Courage as payment for his services as a clerk*

Simplicius asked how Hopalong had gotten involved with her and what she had had to do with him. I answered: "As far as I can still remember, she was his concubine in *Italia* as I have already mentioned, or rather, to all appearances, he was her servant, especially since (if what this slut told me be true) she also gave him the name of Hopalong."

"Quiet, you villain, a plague on you!" said Hopalong. "Quiet, you quill-driver, or by God, I'll lay this candlestick across your skull and see the color of your blood!" And to make good his words he snatched up the candlestick, but Simplicius was just as quick and far stronger than he and was also of a different mind, for which reason he prevented him from striking the blow and threatened to throw him out the window if he did not calm himself; in the meantime the innkeeper came in and ordered us to keep the peace, expressly threatening that if we were not quiet the bailiffs and turnkeys would soon appear to conduct the troublemaker, or perhaps even all three of us, to different lodgings. Now although I straightway began to tremble with fear when I heard this and became as quiet as a mouse, I still did not wish to suffer such insults, but intended to go to the mayor and lodge a complaint in regard to the injury which had been done me; but Simplicius and the innkeeper, the latter of whom had seen Hopalong's ducats and hoped to lay hold of a few of them, consoled me most persuasively so that I changed my mind, although Hopalong kept on growling at me like a vicious old dog. Finally it was agreed that if Hopalong apologised to me I should forgive him for the way he had insulted me, and I should furthermore be the guest of Hopalong and Simplicissimi for as long as I liked.

After this agreement Simplicius asked me how I had gotten away from the so-called gypsies again and in what pursuits they had passed their time in the forest. I answered: "In eating, drinking, sleeping, dancing, fornicating, smoking, singing, wrestling, fencing, and jumping about. The main work of the women was cooking and making fires, except for a few old crones who sat about and instructed the young girls in how to tell fortunes, or rather, how to lie. Some of the men hunted game, without doubt casting a magic spell over it so that it must needs stand still, and it was their practice to kill the game by using spent powder which made no sound when fired off, and I certainly remarked among them no lack of either wild game or domestic animals. We had hardly been camped there two days when again one party after the other began to arrive, among them some whom I had hitherto not yet seen; some (who were of course not kindly received) asked to borrow money from Courage (I guess from the common hoard), but others brought in booty, and none appeared without bringing along either bread, butter, bacon, chickens, geese, ducks, suckling pigs, goats, mutton, or even well-fatted swine, except for one poor old witch who arrived without any booty but a backside beaten black and blue, as she had been caught in a criminal act and rewarded for her pains with ringing cuffs and blows; and I suppose, as is easy to imagine, that they either stole from around the villages and farms the above-mentioned poultry and farm animals or else cut them out of some herd or other; while such companies arrived in our camp daily, some of us also left camp every day, to be sure not always as gypsies, but rather dressed in the manner, I suppose, which was suitable for whatever thievish tricks they had planned; and these, Noble Sir, were the pursuits of the gypsies which I observed for as long as I was with them.

"Now, Noble Sir, since you demand it, I shall tell you how I got away from them again, although my acquaintanceship with Courage does me as little honor as Hopalong's did him or even yours did you, Simplice.

"I was not able to write for more than three or four hours a day, because Courage took no more time than that to dictate to me; and when I was through for the day I was permitted to take walks, play, and amuse myself with the others, whereby all and sundry showed themselves amenable and well-disposed toward me; indeed, Courage herself kept me company most of the time, because these people have in their lives no place at all for any sadness, sorrow, or grief; they reminded me of weasels and foxes, the way they lived in freedom and spent their days stealing, cautious and sly and ready to shake the dust from their heels in an instant whenever they remarked themselves to be in danger. Once Courage asked me how I liked this life of freedom, and I answered: 'Very much!'; and though everything I said was a lie, I even added that I had wished more than once that I could be a gypsy too.

" 'My son,' said she, 'if you have a hankering to stay with us, it can be arranged.'

" 'Yes, Milady,' I answered, 'if only I could speak the language!'

" 'You will soon learn it,' said she, 'I learned it myself in less than six months. If you stay with us, I shall get you a pretty bed-mate to marry up with.'

"I answered that I wished to think it over for a few more days and decide whether I might expect to find a better life any place else; I claimed I had long since tired of studying and sitting over my books night and day, and I did not wish to work either, much less learn a trade; and to top it all I could expect but a niggling *patrimonium* from my parents.

" 'You show great wisdom, my son,' the old crowbait went on, 'and you can see and discern how much better our way of life is, namely, when you consider that not a one of our children would let even the greatest prince take him away and adopt him and make a gentleman of him. Our children count such high princely favors for naught, while other slavish people greatly desire them.'

"I let her think she had won me over, but in my mind I felt about her the same way Hopalong did, for by pretending that I wished to stay with her I hoped to receive permission that much sooner to leave camp with the others and thereby find an opportunity to escape.

"At just this time a band of gypsies arrived, bringing with them a young gypsy maiden who was more beautiful than even the most beautiful of these people generally are; she, as well as other maids, soon became acquainted with me (for you must know that unmarried gypsies, because of their sloth, do not shy away from love-making, nor are they ashamed of it), and she proved to be so friendly, charming, and winning that I believe I should have come to an agreement with her if I had not feared that I should be obliged to learn witchcraft and if I had not but recently heard of Courage's wanton and wicked life from her own lips; for just this reason I was that much more cautious and careful, but I acted more agreeable toward her than toward any other of the gypsy women. Straightway after we had become acquainted she asked me what I was writing down for the 'Countess,'[1] for that is what she called Courage. But when I answered that she had no need to know that, she was quite satisfied with this reply, and I thought I remarked too from the way Courage behaved that she herself had bade the girl ask me this question, to test my discretion, for, or at least so I foolishly thought, she became more and more friendly to me.

"By then I had already gone two weeks without ever once taking off my clothes, for which reason I began to be plagued by lice, which secret suffering I confided to my gypsy lass; at first she laughed mightily at my plight and called me a simple-minded booby; but the next morning she brought me a salve which was supposed to drive all lice away if I would sit naked by the fire, as is the custom of the gypsies, and let someone smear me all over with it, which task the lass herself was willing to perform. But I was much too ashamed to let her do it, and besides, I feared that the same thing might happen to me that had happened to Apulejo,[2] whom a similar treatment had transformed into an ass. But in time the varmints began to torture me so much that I could no longer bear it, for which reason I was forced to make use of this salve treatment, but with the proviso that I would not hold still and let her treat me till I had first greased her all over; to this purpose we made a fire some distance away from our camp and there did as we had agreed to.

"The lice were driven away all right, but the next morning my skin and hair was so black that I looked like the devil himself; I did not know this myself till Courage began to tease me, saying: 'Well, my son, I see that you have already given in to your desire and have become a real gypsy.'

" 'Not that I know of, honored mother,' I answered. But she said: 'Look at your hands,' and with that she had them bring me a mirror, and she pointed to a figure in it which I did not recognize as my own and which frightened me, for it was exceeding black in color.

" 'This salving, my child,' she said, 'means as much to us as circumcision does to the Turks, and the girl who salved you must henceforth be your wife, whether you like her or not.' And with that this Satan's brood began to laugh as if they were about to burst.

"Now when I saw how matters stood I felt like cursing heaven and hell; but what could I do but accommodate myself to the will of those who at that time had me in their power? 'Ha!' I said. 'What do I care? Do you think perhaps that this change grieves me? Stop laughing and tell me instead when my wedding will be.'

" 'Whenever you wish,' Courage answered. 'Whenever you wish, but let us wait till we can have a priest present too.'

"At that time I was already finished with Courage's life history, except that I was supposed to add a few thievish capers, I know not of what sort, which she had perpetrated since she had become a gypsy; therefore I very politely requested the wages I had been promised; but she said: 'Oh, my son, you need no money now; it will come in handy after you have married.' I thought: 'The devil must have given you the idea that you could hold me here this way.' And when she remarked that I was looking somewhat sour she named and appointed me the highest *secretarium* for the Egyptian Nation in all of Germany and promised me that my wedding with her young cousin should take place at the earliest opportunity and that I should receive as dowry two beautiful horses; and so that I might be that much more convinced that this was so, my bride was enjoined to entertain me with her customary amiability.

"Shortly after all this had happened we broke camp, and about thirty of us, including women and children, marched slowly and in good order down the Bühl Valley; for this journey Courage did not wear her splendid costume but rather was dressed like any other old witch; I was with the foragers and helped raid several farms, during which duty I may say that I was no slouch but indeed a leader among the foremost of the gypsies. The next day we marched all the way to the Rhine and spent the night in a thicket near a village where there was a ferry on which we were to cross the Rhine the next day. But in the morning, when the black-skinned *secretarius* awoke, look you, the poor fellow found himself quite alone, for all the gypsies, including his bride, had deserted him completely, so that he had nothing to remember them by except his charming color.''

CHAPTER 7

Simplicissimi Magic Book and the excellent profits he made

"Now there I sat as if God himself had forsaken me, though I had good reason to be grateful to Him that this wanton rabble had not murdered me or stripped me in my sleep and stolen what little money I still carried with me for food. And you, Hopalong, what reason have you now to rage at me, since I am voluntarily relating how I was cheated, as were you, by this vicious slut whose cunning and malice are such that no man can escape them once she has fixed upon him, as was very nearly the case with our honorable Simplicissimo?"

"None," answered Hopalong. "None whatsoever, good friend. Let us forget it, and the devil take that witch!"

"Pray," Simplicius answered him, "Don't wish the poor ninny any worse ill yet; have you not heard that she is close to damnation as it is, up to her ears in the mire of wickedness and sin, if not already in the jaws of hell? Rather say a few reverent *pater nosters* for her sake, that the kindness of God may illuminate her heart and bring her to true repentance!"

"What," said Hopalong, "I'd rather lightning strike her dead."

"Oh, God save us," answered Simplicius, "I assure you that if you persist in this I should not wish to have to say which one of you two will find eternal salvation."

To this Hopalong replied, "What do I care?" But good Simplicius shook his head with a deep sigh. By then it was nigh on to two o'clock in the afternoon, and we had all three eaten more than enough, when Hopalong asked Simplicius how he earned his daily bread and what his position, trade, and livelihood was.

Simplicius answered: "That I shall let you see before the next half-hour has passed." Hardly had he closed his mouth when along the road came his dad and mother, together with a husky farmhand, all of whom were driving before them two pair of fatted oxen, which they put in the stable. Simplicius straightway enjoined his aforementioned two old parents to come in out of the cold and into the warm room, which parents in truth looked the way their picture in Simplicius' *Perpetual Calendar*[1] portrays them. And when the farmhand also came in, Simplicius ordered the innkeeper to bring them food and drink, but he himself took the sack which his farmhand was carrying and said to Hopalong: "Now come with me, and you will see how I earn my daily bread."

To me he said, however, that I might come along with them too if I wished. And so the three of us shuffled to a square full of people to which Simplicius had a table brought, as well as a measure of new wine and a half-dozen empty glasses. It looked as if we intended to hold a drinking bout right there in the open marketplace, in the most bitter cold. Soon we attracted many onlookers, but the audience did not stay because the same terrible cold forced everyone to go away again. This Hopalong noted, and for that reason said to Simplicius: "Brother, do you want me to make these people stay here?"

Simplicius answered: "That trick I know myself, but if you wish to, let's see what you can do."

With that, Hopalong whisked out his fiddle and began to put on a show and at the same time to play the fiddle. He shaped his lips into a triangle, a square, a pentagon, a hexagon, yea, into a heptagon, and while he was playing the fiddle, all the while he made music with his mouth too, as he had done earlier in the inn, but since the fiddle, which had been tuned in the warmth of the room, would not play right in the cold, he imitated all sorts of bird and animal calls, from the lovely forest song of the nightingale to, and including, the frightful howl of the wolf, as a result of which we had attracted in less than a quarter of an hour an audience of more than six hundred people, who looked on wide-eyed and open-mouthed with astonishment, forgetful of the cold.

Simplicius commanded Hopalong to be silent so that he might state his business to the people. When this was done Simplicius said to the audience: "Gentlemen, I am not a barker, a vagabond, a quack, or a doctor; I am an artist! To be sure, I cannot practice sorcery, but my arts are so wondrous that many take them to be magic. That this is not true, however, and that everything I do happens in accordance with the laws of nature can be seen from this book I have here, in which there are sufficient authentic documents and testimonials in support of my claims."

With that he drew a book out of the sack and leafed through it to show the audience his authentic certificates; but, look you, in the book there was nothing but blank pages. "Well!" he said then, "I can see that I am standing here like butter in the sun. Alas!" he said to the audience. "Is there no learned man among you who might blow a few letters into my book for me?"

And since two dandies were standing closest to him, he asked one of them to blow into the book just a little, with the assurance that it would in no wise do harm either to his reputation or to his soul. When the dandy had done this, Simplicius leafed through the book, and now there appeared to be nothing in it but pictures of arms and armor.

"Aha!" he said. "This gentleman likes rapiers and pistols better than books and letters. He will make a better soldier than a doctor. But what shall I do with weapons in my book? They must be gotten rid of!" And with this Simplicius himself blew into the book,[2] as if he were blowing through the pages, and he again showed the audience when he leafed through it nothing but blank pages, at which everyone was amazed.

The other dandy, who was standing next to the first one, asked on his own to blow into the book also. When this was done Simplicius leafed through the book and showed the audience and the dandy pictures of ladies and gentlemen.

"Look you!" said Simplicius. "This gentleman likes to spoon, for he has blown into my book nothing but young swains and maidens. But what shall I do with so many idlers? They are a lot of hungry pawns who do me no good. Away with them!" And then he blew through the book again and showed all the audience, as he leafed through it, nothing but blank pages.

After this Simplicius let a respected citizen from whose appearance one might expect great wealth blow into the book. Afterwards he leafed through the book and showed him and the audience nothing but sovereigns and ducats, saying: "This gentleman either has much money or will soon receive much, or at least wishes to possess a large *summa*. What he blew into the book will be mine." And with that he bade me hold open his sack, in which he had at least three hundred tin boxes. He blew through the book, into the sack, and said: "That is the way to save these fellows." And afterwards he once more showed the audience only blank pages in his book.

Thereupon he let another, one of less wealthy appearance, blow into it, leafed around in the book, and when nothing but dice and playing cards appeared, he said: "This chap likes to gamble, but I do not, and therefore the cards must go." And when he himself had again blown through the book, he once more showed the audience only blank pages.

A buffoon in the audience said that he could read and write and that he ought to blow into it, because he knew that then fine testimonials would appear. "Oh, yes!" said Simplicius. "This honor shall straightway be yours." Holding the book before him, he let him blow as long as he wished, and when this had happened Simplicius leafed through it and showed him and the audience nothing but the heads of hares, asses, and fools, and said: "If you intended to blow into it nothing but your own brethren, then you might just as well have spared yourself the trouble." That caused such laughter as could be heard nine houses away, but Simplicius said that he must again get rid of the varmints, he himself could serve in their stead, and with that he once more blew through the book and showed the audience again, as before, nothing but blank pages. "Alas!" he said. "How glad I am that I have gotten rid of these fools again."

There was one man standing there whose nose glowed like copper, and to him Simplicius said: "Prithee, come blow into this too, to see what you can do." He complied, and when it was done Simplicius showed him and the others nothing but pictures of drinking vessels. "Ha!" said Simplicius. "Here is a man after my own heart. He likes to drink, and I too like to bring a toast!" And with that he tapped with his finger on the pitcher and said further to him: "Look, friend, in this pitcher is a drink to your good health which you shall receive presently." To me, however, Simplicius said that I should fill the glasses one by one, which task I indeed performed. Meanwhile he again blew through the book, once more showed the audience blank pages, and said that this time he could not fill that many drinking vessels, but that he already had glasses enough for his single measure of wine which was there. Finally he let a young student blow into the book, whereupon he leafed through it and showed the audience nothing but pages filled with writing. "Aha!" he said. "There you are at last! Right, gentlemen, these are my authentic testimonials, of which I told you earlier. These I shall leave in the book, and I shall hold this young gentleman here to be a scholar and give him one in return for having helped me to my excellent documents.'' And with this he stuck the book into his sack and ended his display of legerdemain.

But now he had a man from the audience hand him one of the boxes from the sack and said: ''You gentlemen understand that I do not claim to be a doctor, but rather an artist—which I still maintain—but even so, I might be taken for a wine-doctor, for wines too have their illnesses and ailments, all of which I am able to cure. If a certain wine is spoiled, and so ropy that one could wind it up on a spoon like syrup, then before you can count to twenty I can help it so that it will sparkle when poured, and its little bubbles will jump right out of the glass. If it is stale, and red as a fox, in three days I shall bring back its natural color. If it tastes of a mouldy barrel, then in a few days I shall produce in it so much flavor that you will take it for muscatel. If it is as sour as if it had been grown in Bavaria or Hesse, and if, besides, because it is green, or for other reasons, it is so cloudy that it could be used to stop up worm holes, and could be used both as food and drink, as nourishing as beer is in other places, look you, gentlemen, then I shall presently change it so that you will take it to be either Malvoisier or Spanish, or the very best, or at least a good aged wine. And this art, although most incredible, I shall presently put to the test and prove to you, before your very eyes.''

Thereupon he took from the box an amount the size of a pea, put it into a glass full of wine, and stirred it all up together. From this admixture he poured one drop into the first glass, two into the second, three into the third, and four into the fourth, whereupon the wine in the glasses straightway changed to various colors, according to whether he had poured a few or many drops into each one. The fifth glass of wine, however, into which he had not poured anything, remained as it was, that is, a cloudy and raw new wine, for it had been grown just this year. Then he let the most prominent men in the audience taste these wines, all of which persons were amazed at the quick change and the diverse tastes and kinds of wines.

''Yes, gentlemen,'' he continued, ''now that you have seen the proof of this art, you must also know that a pea-sized amount of this elixir into a measure of wine, or a whole boxful like this one into a forty-gallon barrel, would be more than enough to improve the wine to the fullest and to make it equal to Spanish or Malvoisier wine, unless the new wine that you want to improve be all too sour. Anyone who would prefer to drink a delicate wine rather than a sour one may buy some of this elixir from me today, for tomorrow a little box will no longer be sold cheaply for six pence, as it is today, since what I have left tomorrow will perforce cost half a guilder a box. To be sure, this is not because I am in that dire a need of money, but rather because I am purveying this elixir the way Sybilla[3] did her books.''

By that time we had an audience of nigh on to a thousand persons, for the most part grown men, and when the buying began, Simplicius almost did not have enough hands to take in the money and to hand out the boxes. I, for my part, gave out for tasting all the wine we had brought along, which wine Simplicius from time to time improved with his admixture. Before a half-hour was past, he had already turned all his boxes into silver and taken in good hard cash for them, so that he had to let half the people who still wanted to buy them go away empty-handed.

After these transactions he had all the table glasses and the vessels taken back to where they belonged, and after he had paid the owner for the use of them, we went back together to our lodgings, where Simplicius' dad had already sold the four oxen for 130 sovereigns and was ready to count out the money to Simplicius.

''Do you see now,'' Simplicius said to Hopalong, ''how I earn my daily bread?''

''I certainly do!'' answered Hopalong. ''I thought I was a veritable rabbi[4] when it came to making money, but now I well see that you outstrip me by far. Indeed, I believe that with you the devil himself would get the shitty end of the stick.''

CHAPTER 8

Under what conditions Simplicissimus taught his art to Hopalong

"My God, Hopalong!" said Simplicius. "How can you be so foulmouthed?"

"You've not heard anything yet!" answered Hopalong. "I've not said half of what I really think."

"What *do* you really think?" asked the other.

"If you don't mind me saying so," answered Hopalong, "it sure looks to me as if you are very near a wizard, or at least that you had an excellent teacher."

"And I," said Simplicius, "am of the opinion, and also firmly believe, that you are a complete ass, and moreover learned your trade from no teacher whatsoever. Prithee! What cause do I give you to think so ill of me?"

"I have seen enough of your tricks today," answered Hopalong.

Simplicius, for his part answered: "It is most certainly a disgrace that you, at your advanced age, having wandered around this earth so long, are still so simple-minded that you take for magic and sorcery perfectly natural works of art and science, such as you saw when I improved the wine, and childish tricks, of which you saw an example today in my book."[1]

"Yes," said Hopalong. "But it is not only that. I see that money simply rains down on you, whereas I am obliged to put forth such great effort and labor for every penny I earn, and if I want to have and keep a supply of them, I am obliged to skimp and scrape."

"You dreamer!" said Simplicius. "Do you think I come by my money without lifting a finger or raising an eyebrow? My old folks were obliged to spend money and effort to raise and fatten those four oxen, but I too was obliged to labor to manufacture the *materiam* which I turned into cash today."

"But what about the book?" asked Hopalong. "Wasn't that witchcraft? Wasn't that a bit of white magic?"

Simplicius answered: "What about the tricks of jugglers and conjurers? They are childish tricks and tomfoolery which amaze you simple boobies only because your crude minds cannot grasp them!"

After a lengthy exchange in this vein, Hopalong finally declared that Simplicius was lucky if he were able to perform such tricks in a natural way, and offered him twenty sovereigns if he would teach him to conjure and tell fortunes with the book. "For, dear brother," he said, "I am obliged to earn my daily bread by begging and playing my fiddle, and don't you know that it would prove most profitable to me at country fairs or weddings if I were able to amuse and amaze my listeners with this cunning little trick? Wouldn't I harvest ten times more coins than if I only played my fiddle and engaged in my jokes and jests?"

"My friend," answered Simplicius, "it would be a good thing if you left off completely from your jokes and jests, as you call them. For look you, you are in fact a man of seventy,[2] who already has one foot in the grave, and surely is not safe from death at any hour. Moreover, you have, as I have seen, a goodly amount of money, on which you can live quite comfortably as long as God permits. If I were in your shoes, I should retire so that I should be able to contemplate the life I had led, repent of the sins I had committed, find my way back to God, and serve only Him henceforth, which way of life could be pursued in a hospice, where you might buy bed and board, or perhaps in a monastery, where you might serve as a gatekeeper. We rage and tempt God more than enough when we cling to the world's follies on into our old age, pitching and wallowing in all manner of sins and vices, like a sow in the mire. But it is still worse, and even greater folly, if we persist in this to the end of our days, and do not give a thought to our salvation or damnation, much less to mending our ways."

"I should be a fool," answered Hopalong, "to stick the money which I scraped together with great effort and labor into a hospice or a monastery, and thus pay to be robbed of my freedom."

Simplicius said in response: "And you are being a fool if you think that you are enjoying your supposed freedom, but are actually remaining a servant of sin, a slave to the devil, and thus, alas, an enemy also of God. I cleave to my aforesaid opinion, namely, that it would be both advisable and beneficial to you to mend your ways before the sleep of eternal night and darkness overcomes you. For look you, day is ending for you twenty years before it will end for me, and your late evening should remind you that soon you will go to sleep."

Hopalong answered: "Brother, you take twenty sovereigns from me for the art I wish to learn, and let the priests preach to them as likes to listen to 'em. In return, I'll promise you that I shall in fact keep in mind what you have just said."

Now just as there is nothing in the whole wide world so vain and useless that it cannot be employed and used to some good purpose, so Simplicius in fact proposed to use his book, which he called his "Magic Book" to convert Hopalong, for which reason Simplicius said to him: "Tell me, friend, did you seriously believe that it was witchcraft, or at least white magic, when you saw me practice my art with the book in the marketplace?"

Hopalong answered: "Yes! And I should still believe it, if I had not heard you speak so piously just now."

"Now then," said Simplicius, "keep in mind till the end of your days this speech and this illusion which has deceived you, and promise me that whenever you use this book you will always remember what I shall tell you further. Do that, and not only shall I initiate you into this supposed art for nothing, without taking the twenty sovereigns you offered me, but on top of that I shall also give you the book in the bargain, for without it you will not be able to practice this art."

Hopalong asked what things he should remember every time he used the book, and Simplicius answered: "First of all, when you show the audience nothing but white pages, remember that God in holy baptism has given you back the white garment of innocence, which, however, you have since befouled so often with all manner of sins. Then, when you show the weapons of war, remember how reprehensibly and how godlessly you have spent your life making war. Then, when you get to the pictures of money, remember how you exposed your body and soul to danger by chasing after it; and at the sight of the drinking vessels, remember also your past swinish drinking bouts, and at the sight of the dice and playing cards, think how much valuable time and how many valuable hours you have wasted with them, what cheating took place during these games, and with what frightful blasphemies the Almighty was dishonored during them. At the sight of the swains and maidens, remember your own whoremongering, and when you get to the fools' heads, believe firmly that those without doubt are fools who let themselves be deceived and robbed of their eternal salvation by the allurements of the world enumerated above. But when you show the writing in the book, remember that Holy Scripture does not lie when it says that the avaricious, the envious, the wrathful, the quarrelers, the brawlers and murderers, the gamblers, the drunkards, the whoremongers and adulterers will hardly come into the Kingdom of Heaven, and that therefore any man is a fool if he lets himself be seduced by these vices, and deprived so disgracefully of his salvation. Now even though most, and indeed the simplest, of your spectators may think that they are being tricked by you, which is in fact not true, you should consider and bear in mind that the Devil and Dame World use the aforementioned vices to trick and blind most of these ignorant people, unbeknownst to themselves, thereby leading them into eternal damnation.''

"Brother," Hopalong then said, "that is really too much! Who, in the name of St. Peter, can keep all these things in his head?"

Simplicius answered: "My friend, if you cannot do that, then you will not be able to remember how to handle the book right either!"

"Oh no!" answered Hopalong. "That I'll learn all right!"

"And the book," answered Simplicius, "will help to remind you of what you ought to remember for my sake, or rather, for your own."

"I'd rather give you the twenty sovereigns," said Hopalong, "and be rid of this obligation."

Simplicius answered: "But Simplicius is not willing to do this, not only because the book and the art of using it are not worth that much money without the things which I want you to remember, but also because Simplicius' conscience will not let him take a single penny from you, since he does not know how you have earned or otherwise come by your money. In fact, I shall not give you the book unless you promise to remember always what I have told you, even if you were to pay me a hundred sovereigns cash for it."

Hopalong scratched his head and said: "You are almost awakening fearful thoughts in me. I see that you desire neither your own profit nor my loss, but *ma foi,* brother, there is something behind all this which I do not understand! From the fact that you do not want to harm me by taking my money, I can tell that you wish me well, and that the command to remember those things, which I took to be a heavy burden, you put on me for my own good; for which reason I herewith promise to remember everything you have asked of me, in return for this art.''

Thereupon Simplicius took out the book and showed Hopalong all the tricks of using it. And since they let me watch too, I found out exactly how it was made, so that I could right off make one like it myself, which in fact I did do a few days later, in order to make this Simplician ''Magic Book''[3] available to the whole world.

CHAPTER 9

Table talk and nocturnal discourse, and why Hopalong did not want to have a wife

While this discourse and transaction was going on between Simplicius and Hopalong, the time for the evening repast approached. I wanted to order my meal separately, but Simplicius said that both I and Hopalong must be his guests—Hopalong, of course, because he was an old comrade-in-arms and a newly acquired apprentice, I, however, because I had today brought him such pleasing news, namely, that his son Simplicius had not been born to that wanton, Courage. Moreover, he said it was only fitting that he reimburse me both for my clerk's wages and for whatever else I had suffered on his account at the hands of the gypsies. Now while we were thus talking with one another, young Simplicius, who was at that time studying in this city and had heard of his father's arrival, came to the inn, together with one of his fellow scholars. He too was a tall, gigantic fellow, in every way like his father, and he looked so much like him in the face that anyone, even if he had not known it, would have guessed without difficulty that he was Simplicius' natural son, in spite of the fact that that miserable Courage imagined that she had deceived him so masterfully with a changeling.

Thus there were sitting at the table Simplicius' dad and mother, old and young Simplicius, together with the latter's comrade, the student whom he had brought along, myself, Hopalong, and Simplicius' farmhand. The meal was good, and short, because the two old folks hied themselves off to bed, for they said that even though they would not be able to sleep, the rest would do them good anyhow. And therefore there was all the less conversation. One thing did happen from which I gathered that Hopalong's memory and ability to grasp something quickly was not really faulty at all; for when the aforementioned student desired to see Simplicius' book, which he had heard described as something quite miraculous by someone who had seen Simplicius perform with it in the marketplace, he had young Simplicius ask his father whether he might not have the honor of seeing it. But old Simplicius answered that he did not have it in his possession any more, but he told Hopalong to show the two students what he had learned today. Hopalong straightway took out the book and, leafing through it and showing the students the blank pages, said: "As clean and unmarked as this blank white paper your souls were created and came into this world, and therefore your parents have sent you here (with these words he pointed to the written pages) to study and learn the Scripture. But you fellows, instead of acquiring worthwhile knowledge, are wont to spend and waste your money (here he pointed to the pictures of the various coins) on drinking (here he pointed to the drinking vessels), on gambling (here the playing cards and dice), on whoring (here the swains and maidens), and on brawling (here the weapons). But I say to you that all who do such things are naught but such fellows as you see here with your own eyes," and thereby he showed them the heads of the fools, hares, and asses. And with that he whisked the book back into his poke. This performance so pleased old Simplicius that he told Hopalong that if he had known that he would learn this art so quickly and well, he would not have asked of him half so large an apprentice's fee.

As mentioned before, we did not tarry long over the evening meal, during the course of which I observed how kindly Simplicius honored and treated his parents, and how they in turn honored and treated him and his son in the same way. One saw and felt nothing but love and good faith, and although each held the other in the highest regard, one did not notice any fear in any of them; rather each showed genuine love and affection for the other. Young Simplicius knew how to behave most politely towards all, and the farmhand—and people of that ilk are usually crude churls—displayed more breeding and good manners than many a fellow of better birth who has had his own *praeceptor* to teach him *mores*, with the result that I wondered how Simplicissimus, who had formerly been so crude and godless, had been able to put his household on such a reputable footing, and to teach his family and servants, who were as simple as they were uncouth, such laudable manners and morals.

Hopalong was very quiet, I know not whether because he was as surprised as I was, or because he was meditating on the secrets to be found in Simplicius' "Magic Book," which secrets, to my way of thinking, were causing him to think all sorts of things. One thing was for sure: rarely have such diversely clad people sat down to eat at the same table. Simplicius' dad looked like a respected old village mayor, his mother like the mayor's wife, the farmhand like their son, old Simplicius as I have described him above in the second chapter, young Simplicius and his comrade like two dandies, Hopalong like a beggar, and I myself like a poor quill-driver, or like a *praeceptor,* in my shiny black coat.

We were all lodged in one room, because that is the way Simplicius wanted it, and because Hopalong assured the innkeeper that he did not have lice. Simplicius and Hopalong each slept by himself, while the rest of us slept together in pairs—Simplicius' dad and mother, the two *studiosi,* and I and the farmhand, who gave me so much trouble with the covers that despite the terrible cold I was not able to keep my nose under the blankets much that night. Old Simplicius, however, demonstrated by his snores that he could sleep as well as he could digest food and drink in large quantities. Now inasmuch as we went to bed quite early, a good part of the long winter night remained which we were not able to spend sleeping. Simplicius' dad and mother awoke first, and when he began to cough and she to chatter with him, all the rest of us woke up. Now when Simplicius noticed that Hopalong was also awake, he began to talk with him, recalling the times when they were comrades-in-arms, and what had happened to the two of them here and there. This led Simplicius to ask Hopalong how he had fared since then; where he had since been tramping about in the world; where his fatherland was; whether he did not have any relatives there, or perhaps a wife and child, or perhaps a household of his own somewhere; why he was wandering about in such wretched rags, when the whole time he had a heap of money with him, etc.

"Alas, brother!" answered Hopalong. "If I were obliged to tell you all that, the remaining seven hours of this long night would be much too short. I was indeed in my fatherland recently, but just as I have never owned anything there, so it offered me no shelter this time either, but rather made clear to me the character of my condition, namely, that I should continue to wander about like fleet-footed *Mercurius.* And if I did not meet any relatives there, however far removed, much less any brothers or other close friends, and if indeed almost no one could remember my step-father, in whose fatherland I very diligently inquired about him and his friends, then how should I have been able to find out anything about the family of my real father and mother, when I do not even rightly know where they were born? And since you can easily gather from this that I have no home to call my own, you can easily surmise that I have neither wife nor children. And besides, dear friend, why should I burden myself with a pack of troubles? But that I hang on to my money is the right thing to do, since I know both how hard it is to obtain it and how consoling it is in lonely and worrisome old age. And, finally, that I go about dressed so poorly is not without good reason either, since my trade and my clients demand that I wear these rags, and even worse ones.''

''I should nevertheless have thought,'' answered Simplicius, ''that if I were in your shoes it would be better to have a wife who, by virtue of conjugal love and devotion, would be a helpmeet and counsel in my frail old age, than to crawl about in misery this way, forsaken by everyone. How do you think you will fare if you should perchance become bedridden sometime or other?''

''Ah, brother,'' said Hopalong, ''that's a shoe that doesn't fit me. For if I had a wife who was old, I should perchance be obliged to doctor more on her than she on me. If she were young, I should be no more than her cover for her sin and shame. If she were middle-aged, she might perchance be spiteful and shrewish. If she were rich, she would treat me with contempt. If she were poor, I might think that she married me only for my few pennies, let alone that anyone can easily figure out that no woman worth her salt would take a pegleg for a husband.''

''Now, now!'' answered Simplicius. ''If you fear every thorn, you'll never pluck a rose.''

''Well, brother,'' said Hopalong, ''if you knew how much I have suffered at the hands of one woman, you would not be astonished that, like a child, I am 'once burnt, twice shy.' ''

Simplicius asked: ''You mean perchance that frivolous Courage?''

''Not at all!'' answered Hopalong. ''With her I lived the life of a lord, despite the fact that she kicked over the traces, as it were, in public. But what did I care? After all, she was not my lawfully wedded wife.''

''Fie on you!'' said Simplicius. ''Pray don't talk so crudely and immodestly. Remember that you are in the company of respectable folk. But listen, just because one woman deceived you, do you think that there is not a single decent woman left in the world who would live with you in honor and good faith?''

Hopalong answered: "That I don't deny. But on the other hand, it is certain that a husband is obliged to pay dearly enough for any good a wife does him. The things a wife does best of all cost her husband dearly enough, because what the husband has earned with the sweat of his brow is most often wasted unnecessarily. If I have a wife, then nothing is more certain than that each of my ducats will henceforth be worth no more than a sovereign. If she spins a piece of cloth to make clothes for me and herself, I must pay for the flax, wool, and the weaver. If she is going to cook something for me, then I must provide the food, the wood, the salt, and the lard, together with the pots and pans. If she desires to bake for me, who but I must supply the flour? Moreover, who pays for wood, soap, and washerwoman when she wants to have her linen and mine washed? And how about when a man is burdened with a pack of children? To be sure, I have no experience in this, and do not desire to have any either. Namely, when one child is sickly, the second healthy, the third lazy, the fourth willful, the fifth doltish, and the sixth fractious, disobedient, and no-account?"

Simplicius answered: "You are just an old dodderer, and you do not deserve a decent wife, otherwise you would speak far differently about holy matrimony, which was ordained by God Himself and blessed with many promises of good. And simply because a good and virtuous wife is a gift of God and the crown and ornament of man, it vexes you that gracious Heaven has not found you worthy of such a spouse."

"Sure, Simplicius," answered Hopalong, "you are a fine one to talk!"

CHAPTER 10

Hopalong's origins and how he first went to war

"Well, that is enough talk about womenfolk," said Simplicius, "particularly since I can see that I cannot persuade you to change your mind or to marry. But nevertheless, I should like to hear from you whence you came, how you went to war, and how you fared there, and how it happened that such a brave soldier ended up such a wretched gimp."

Hopalong answered: "Since you did not hesitate to put your own life story in print for all the world to see, I shall not be ashamed to tell you mine here in the dark, particularly since what happened betwixt me and Courage—through whom, so I hear, you and I are kinsmen—must already be public knowledge. Now listen, and I shall tell you of your kinsman's origins. My mother was a Peloponnesian Greek of an old and noble family and of great wealth; my real father, however, was an Albanian juggler and acrobat, and of low birth and little means in the bargain. When he was wandering about with a tame lion and a dromedary in the region where my mother's parents lived, earning money by exhibiting both these animals and his own art, his physical proportions and carriage so pleased my mother, then a young thing of seventeen, that she was straightway smitten with him and, with the help of her nurse, plotted to snitch some money from her parents and, without their knowledge and consent, to run off with him, my father. And in this she succeeded, to her misfortune, albeit they were legally wed. And so, from a lady who resided in splendor and wealth my mother became an itinerant actress, my father a near-nobleman, and I myself the first and only fruit of this first marriage, since my father, straightway after I was born, fell from a tightrope and broke his neck, which grievous fall too soon made my mother a widow.

"She did not have the heart to return home to her irate parents; at any rate, by this time she was more than a hundred miles away with a company of actors in Dalmatia. But she was beautiful, young, and wealthy, and therefore had many suitors from among my late father's comrades. The man whom she permitted to win her hand was a Slovenian by birth and the most skilled artist in the profession which my father had pursued. This man raised me till I reached my eleventh year and taught me all the *principia* of his art, such as how to blow the trumpet, beat the drum, play the fiddle and the pipes (both the shawm and the bagpipes), how to do sleight-of-hand tricks, to jump through hoops, and do other strange and clownish things; thus anyone could easily see that these things were innate to me, rather than things which I had picked up or acquired through diligent instruction. At the same time I learned to read and write and to speak Greek from my mother and Slovenian from my father. I also picked up some German in Styria, Carinthia, and other German border provinces. And, *in summa summarum,* I soon became such a fine amusing juggler boy that my aforementioned father, rather than do without me in his business, would not have sold me for a thousand ducats, even if he had had the chance to every day.

"Thus, in my salad days we tramped about for the most part in Dalmatia, Slovenia, Macedonia, Serbia, Bosnia, Walachia, Transylvania, Russia, Poland, Lithuania, Moravia, Bohemia, Hungary, Styria and Carinthia. And when we had earned a lot of money in these countries and my step-father was agreeable to visiting his wife's parents— before whom he did not hesitate to appear, since he regarded himself as a very wealthy fellow and could comport himself like a count—look you, he betook himself from Istria into Croatia and Slavonia, and from there traveled through Dalmatia and Albania and *per Graeciam* to the Peloponnesus, where my mother's parents lived.

"Now when we were passing through Dalmatia my father wished to let the famous city of Ragusa witness his artistry, or rather to take a pretty penny in plunder from that city, which at that time was in full flourish and riches. We stopped there for this purpose, but in fact did not stay in a church but, as was our wont, in the very best inn. And when we had rested but a night my step-father went to obtain a license to show both his strange animals and his art to the public for money. It was granted, and almost before it had been received, I, together with my step-brother, who did not compare with me by far in dexterity in our art or in other ways, was sent with a hoop, a juggler's bag, and other instruments, to see whether I might not earn a bit of money on the ships which were lying in the harbor. I obeyed with pleasure, thinking to amuse and entertain the sailors and seafarers with my gamboling and juggler's stunts, but alas, I came to a place which was the beginning of all my misery, woe, and discontent; for several ships were riding at anchor outside the harbor, ready to sail and merely waiting for a favorable wind to transport to Spain some newly recruited troops, among them two companies of Albanian lancers,[1] look you, we came unawares on board these ships, since we had been persuaded by one of their boatmen that there we should receive excellent gratuities, and especially since the boatman was willing to row us out to them. We had barely begun our *exercitia*[2] when from the north a wind arose suitable to run before out of the Adriatic into the Sea of Sicily; and to this wind they set their sails after weighing anchor, and taught me and my brother seamanship against our will. My brother acted as if he were about to despair, but I consoled myself, not simply because by nature I was wont to take everything in my stride, but because one of the captains of horse, who had become wholly enamored of the suppleness of my body, promised me mountains of gold, as it were, if I were to stay with him and serve as his page. What was I to do? I could well imagine that no ship would put back to port on our account, nor would the Ragusians give chase to these ships for the sake of two kidnapped juggler boys and, if they were not handed over, engage in a sea battle or start a war. Therefore I submitted to my fate all the more patiently and enjoyed it better than my brother did, who grieved to such a degree that he died before we left *Sicilia,* where we took aboard some more footsoldiers.

"From there we sailed to Milan and then overland through Savoy, Burgundy, and Lorraine, on to Luxemburg and into the Spanish Netherlands, where we, together with numerous other troops, under the command of the famous Ambrosio Spinola,[3] fought against the enemies of the King.[4] At that time I was still rather well contented. I was still young, my master loved me and let me do whatever I wanted to do, I was fatigued by neither forced marches nor other martial labor, and I had not yet made the acquaintance of John Rumblygut,[5] who at that time was not as well known by far to our *soldateska* as he later became in the German war, when even colonels and general officers got to know him well."

CHAPTER 11

Concerning three noteworthy wastrels: true accounts

"Those who go to war generally fare about the same as those who learn witchcraft. For just as the latter, once they have fallen in with such an accursed congregation, are scarcely ever, or even never, able to escape from it, so most soldiers have no desire to leave the war when things are going well, and are generally not able to escape from it when things are going badly. Of those who must abide in war against their own will till they either fall in battle or croak in some other way, or are ruined, or even starve to death, it might be maintained that this was their *fatum* or destiny. But of those who take rich booty and then waste it needlessly it might be said that gracious Heaven does not allow them to make proper use of their good fortune, but rather verifies the old saw 'easy come, easy go' and 'here today, gone tomorrow.'

"I know of three common soldiers who also serve as three different memorable examples to confirm this, and of these I must tell in greater detail. First: Tilly,[1] the famous general, after he had robbed the city of Magdeburg of her maidenhead and his subordinates had robbed her of her finery and wealth too, learned that one of his common soldiers had seized a great amount of money, consisting of coins of many denominations, and had straightway lost it playing dice. In order to learn the truth of the matter, he had this soldier come before him, and after he was given to understand by this unlucky gamester himself that the *summa* he had first seized and then wasted was larger than he had been told by others (some actually said it was thirty thousand ducats, others said it was more), General Tilly said to him: 'You would have had enough money for the rest of your life, and you could have lived like a lord if you had only given yourself the chance. But since you are of no use or any good to yourself, I cannot see how you can hope to be of any use to the Emperor.' And with this the general, who otherwise enjoyed the reputation of treating his soldiers like his own sons, came to the conclusion that this fellow should no longer unnecessarily encumber the earth,

but swing free and easy above it in the air, which sentence was in fact
straightway carried out.

"Second: When the Swedish general, Königsmarck,[2] seized by surprise the sections of Prague on the left bank of the Moldau, and a
common soldier in the same way laid hold of more than twenty thousand
ducats in specie but lost them at the gaming table again at one sitting,
news of this came to the ears of Königsmarck, who likewise had this
soldier brought before him, first to look at him, and then, after deter-
mining the truth of the rumor, to try him the same way Tilly had tried
the other soldier. And when he admonished him, just as Tilly had, and
the soldier noted his general's sober countenance, he said with bold
resolution: 'Your Excellency cannot in fairness have me hanged for
losing the money, because I have hopes of seizing even more booty
when we take the rest of Prague.' This answer, which was taken as a
good omen, did indeed save the fellow's life, but he did not take the
booty he hoped for, nor did the Swedes take the city,[3] which at that time
was hard pressed by their army.

"Third: Anyone who is acquainted with Holtz'[4] infantry regiment in
the army of the Elector of Bavaria has without doubt probably either
seen, or at least heard of, the man called 'Commander Trampius.'[5] He
was a musketeer in the aforementioned regiment, and shortly before
peace was declared he was carrying a pike.[6] I saw him in this state
myself in that same regiment during the armistice;[7] as a matter of fact,
he was so poorly dressed that his shirttails were hanging out of his pants
in front and in back. In the battle of Herbsthausen[8] he got his hands on
such booty, in the shape of a keg full of French doubloons, that he could
hardly carry them, much less count them, nor in fact know and reckon
from their number how great his wealth at that time actually was! But
what did this shiftless Trampius do when he failed to realize how great
his good fortune was? He proceeded to a Bavarian city and fortress[9]
which earlier had caused the great Gustavus Adolphus to clench his
teeth in anger, because after so many splendid victories he had been
obliged to withdraw without taking it. There Trampius decked himself
out like a baron and lived every day like a prince who has an income of
several millions a year. He kept two coachmen, two lackeys, two pages,
and a *valet-de-chambre* in beautiful livery, and after he had provided
himself with a coach and six beautiful horses he traveled across the
Danube to the capital[10] of that same country, where he stopped at the

best inn, spent his time eating, drinking, and taking pleasure trips every day, and gave himself a new name, that is, Commander Trampius. This lordly life lasted about six weeks, during which time his own and real commander, General von Holtz, came there too and stopped at the same inn, since he had there a particularly fine room in which he was wont to lodge whenever he came to town. The innkeeper told him straightway that a foreign cavalier was occupying his usual lodgings and that he dared not ask him to move since he was spending a goodly amount of money at the inn. This brave general was also much too discreet to discommode another guest, but inasmuch as he knew better than the great Atlas[11] all the highways and byways, forests and fields, mountains and valleys, passes and rivers, as well as all the noble families of the Holy Roman Empire, he inquired after the name of this cavalier. And when he heard that the cavalier called himself Commander Trampius, and when he himself was unable to recall any old and noble family or any soldier of fortune[12] by that name, he grew eager to make the acquaintance of this cavalier and to converse with him. He asked the innkeeper about the cavalier's qualities, and when he learned that Trampius, although very sociable, of a merry humor, and generosity personified, was nevertheless a man of few words, the general's eagerness to know this man became all the greater, for which reason he arranged with the innkeeper to obtain Trampius' consent to dine at his table that very evening.

"Commander Trampius was most agreeable to this, and during the sweetmeats course had his servant bring a bowl containing five hundred new French pistoles and a golden chain worth one hundred ducats. 'May it please Your Excellency,' he said to his commanding officer, 'to make do with this small token of my esteem and to remember me fondly.' General von Holtz was astonished at these proffered gifts and answered that he did not know what he might have done or what he might do in the future to deserve such presents from Commander Trampius, for which reason it did not behoove him to accept them. But Trampius begged him not to refuse him, saying that he hoped the time would soon come when His Excellency would himself realize that he was obliged to do him this honor and he, Trampius, then hoped to receive in turn from His Excellency a favor which, to be sure, would not cost him a penny, but which would nevertheless show that these gifts had been well bestowed. Inasmuch as gifts are rejected even less often than they are proffered, von Holtz did not resist any longer, but accepted both the chain and the money (since Trampius insisted that he do so) with courteous promises to repay the favor whenever the opportunity should arise.

"After the general's departure Trampius continued to squander his money. He never passed a guard post without tossing a dozen or at least a half-dozen sovereigns to the sentries, who presented arms in his honor, and he acted this way everywhere he had the opportunity to show that he was a wealthy man. Every day he entertained guests, and every day he paid the innkeeper, never holding back a single penny or complaining about a bill that was too high. But just as any well will eventually run dry, all his money too was soon spent, and in fact, as I have already mentioned, in six weeks' time. Thereupon he turned his coach and his horses into silver. That money too was soon spent. Finally his fine clothes and white linen went the same way, and all that money was also soon consumed. And when his servants saw that things were going downhill for him, one of them after another took his leave, and with his full permission. In the end, when he had nothing left at all but the clothes on his back, and poor clothes at that, with neither a penny nor a farthing in his pockets, the innkeeper gave him fifty sovereigns (because he had spent so much money at the inn) for travel expenses. But he did not budge from the spot till these too had all been spent. The innkeeper, either because he had fleeced him so well or had overcharged him and therefore had a bad conscience, or for some other reason, once more gave him twenty-five sovereigns, with the request that he take these and be gone. But he did not go till he had also used up all this money. And when he was again penniless, the innkeeper once more gave him ten sovereigns to spend for food and lodging on his journey, but Trampius said that since it was money for food and lodging, he would rather spend it there than at another inn, and he did not stop till every last penny of it was gone; which caused the innkeeper to have strange and frightening thoughts, so that he once more gave him five sovereigns to get rid of him. And whereas he had formerly addressed him as 'Your Grace' and had welcomed him most subserviently, now he was obliged to treat him like an inferior if he was to be rid of him; for when he saw that Trampius intended to spend these last five sovereigns at his inn also, he forbade the servants to serve him anything at all. Now when Trampius was forced in this way to quit this inn, look you, he went to another one and there completely extinguished with beer this last spark of his once great fortune. After this he went back to Heilbronn to his regiment, where he was straightway clapped in irons and told that he might be hanged, because he had been absent without leave from the regiment for eight weeks. Now if good old Commander Trampius wished to rid himself of his chains and shackles and the danger of the rope as well, he could do naught but make himself known to his commanding officer, on whom he had bestowed for this very reason such splendid gifts, and who indeed straightway had him freed of both his fetters and his fears. However, he severely admonished him for having needlessly wasted so much money, whereupon Trampius answered in his own defense only that all his life he had wished for nothing more than to know how it felt to be a great lord who wanted for nothing, and this he had come to know by means of his booty.''

CHAPTER 12

*Hopalong becomes a drummer boy,
then a musketeer;* item: *how a peasant
teaches him witchcraft*

When Hopalong had ended the above story about the three famous wastrels and paused a bit, Simplicissimus said: "The last one, to be sure, behaved foolishly enough, but nevertheless more wisely than the other two. And I can imagine no greater human folly than when a man who has much money begins to gamble with one who has little. But in recounting these tales you got off the track of your own life story, which I heartily desire to hear. You stopped when you were with the Spanish army in the Netherlands. How did you fare there?"

Hopalong answered: "I can only say 'quite well,' for if I were to compare this war to the later one, I should have to say that the first one was golden and the other iron.[1] In the first war the soldiers were paid and used to fight, but their lives were not needlessly endangered; but in the other one they were left unpaid, countries were ruined, and both peasant and soldier fell prey to the sword and to hunger, so that in the end there was nothing left to fight with."

Simplicius interrupted him and said: "Either you are talking in your sleep or wish to get off the track again. You are trying to compare two wars and are forgetting once more your own person. Tell us instead how you yourself fared."

"I must be permitted to go into details," answered Hopalong, "when I think of those good old days and at the same time remember the misery which followed. However, my *historia* is as follows: I went with the Spanish to the lower Palatinate when Ambrosius Spinola overran that happy land like the Deluge,[2] and in a short time subjugated God only knows how many cities. There I led such a dissolute life that I fell ill from it and was left behind sick at Worms (to which town Don Gonzales de Cordoba[3] had retreated after he had been obliged to raise the siege of Frankenthal because of the arrival of Mansfeld,[4] whom Tilly had chased

49

across the Rhine at Mannheim). There the fortunes of war played their first malicious prank on me, for, because I had nothing to eat I was obliged to beg and to listen to many a word of abuse. But as soon as I had regained my strength a little, I let two fellows persuade me to go with them to join Tilly's army,[5] which we reached by a short cut just as it was marching on Wiesloch,[6] against Mansfeld's army and at the same time to its own misfortune.

"At that time I was a tall lad of seventeen,[7] and although I was not yet thought capable of being among *tirones*,[8] you could not have found a better drummer boy; and that is what I became and remained, as long as I let them use me thus. To be sure, we suffered at that time a few blows, but they were nothing compared to what we dealt out later in return at Wimpfen.[9] At Wiesloch our regiment did not even get into the battle because it was with the rear guard, but at Wimpfen it proved its valor all the more bravely. I myself did something extraordinary at that time: I slung my drum on my back, took in its stead a dead soldier's musket and bandoleer, and fought in the very front rank in such fashion that not only my captain but my colonel too were obliged to permit me to fight as a soldier. And in so doing I won at that time not only booty, but also a considerable reputation, so that I was even permitted to lay my drum aside for good and carry a musket from then on.

"While with this regiment I helped to defeat the Duke of Brunswick at the Main River,[10] *item* at Stadtlohe,[11] and then finally went with it to the Danish war in Holstein,[12] without yet showing any down on my chin or any wound on my body. And after I had helped defeat the King himself at Lutter,[13] I was used, young as I was, to help take Steinbruck, Verden, Langwedel, Rothenburg, Ottersberg, and various other towns;[14] and finally, because of my good behavior and also because of the favor which my officers showed me, I was assigned *salva guardi*[15] for a long time in a wealthy town, where both I and my purse grew fat. And in this regiment I also acquired three odd nicknames. First, they called me the 'Farter General,'[16] because while I was still a drummer boy I was able, while lying on a bench, to blow or trumpet taps with my arsehole for a whole hour on end, or even longer. Secondly, I was called 'Seyfried with the Horny Skin,'[17] because once, using a broad sword which I swung with both hands, I had fought off three fellows all by myself, and I cut them up badly too. The third name was hung on me by a thieving peasant because of a ridiculous prank which I played on him, with the result that the first two nicknames were forgotten, and everyone henceforth called me 'The Exorcist.'

"It happened like this. Once when I was riding convoy for some horse traders with Frisian horses from our garrison to another one and was not able to return home the same day, I spent the night with the aforementioned peasant, with whom a few other fellows from our regiment were also quartered and who that very day had butchered a pair of fat hogs. He did not have any extra beds, or a warm room either, as is usual in that part of the country, for which reason I slept in the hay, after he had fed me various kinds of freshly cooked sausages. These tasted so good that I could not go to sleep, but instead lay awake and cogitated on how I might get my hands on the butchered hogs themselves. And since I well knew where they were hanging, I went to the trouble of getting up and carrying one side of pork after another into an outbuilding, where I hid them under the straw, thinking that I should fetch them the next night with the help of my comrades. In the morning at daybreak I bade a fond farewell to the peasant and his sons—that is, the soldiers who were quartered with him—and I went my way. But the peasant arrived at the garrison at the same time as I myself did and complained to me that two hogs had been stolen from him the night before.

" 'What!' said I. 'You scoundrel, are you calling me a thief?' And I made such horrible faces that the poor ninny became scared and frightened, especially when I asked him if he would like me to give him a beating. Now since he could easily imagine what the outcome would be if he accused me of having done what I had indeed done, and what in fact no one else could have done, but which he could not prove I had done, this sly *vocativus* tried another tack and said: 'Honored sir! I'd nay think ye capable o' doin' me no harm. Wha' I'm meanin' is that I've hear'd tell that some soldier laddies ha' learnt the art o' makin' such things reappear. If ye can be doin' that for me, then I'll gie ye two sovereigns.'

"I thought the matter over, and since, after all, fighting was not permitted in our garrison, I soon figured out how I could trick him out of the two sovereigns, and for that reason I said to the peasant: 'Old man, that's different. Ask my commanding officer to give me permission to go home with you, and I'll see what I can do.' He was satisfied with that and went with me straightway to my corporal, who was all the more willing to let me go because he saw when I winked at him that I intended to cheat the peasant. For we had nothing else to do in our garrison but to amuse ourselves, since we had chased the King of Denmark from the field and had successfully concluded all of our sieges, with the consequence that at that time we were ruling peacefully over the entire Cymbrian *Cheronesum*, [18] that is, everything that lies between the Baltic and the Atlantic, between Norway, the Elbe River, and the Weser River.

"Upon our arrival at the peasant's cottage we found the table already set, laden with salt pork, a piece of cold salted beef, smoked ham, knackwurst, and such foods, as well as a good draught of Hamburg beer. I, however, preferred first to practice my art and then to gorge myself, to which end I took out my sword and scratched two circles, one inside the other, in the middle of the floor, and several pentagrams betwixt them, and other crazy signs and symbols that came to mind. And when I was finished with that, I said to the people standing about that anyone who was afraid or inclined to fright and therefore did not dare to look upon the devil and his grandmother in person might better leave the room. Thereupon everyone left me except a Bohemian who was also quartered with the peasant, and he stayed with me more because he wished to learn witchcraft, if only he could find someone to teach it to him, than because he was more courageous than the others. We were locked and bolted in, so that no one at all might hinder us in our work, and after I had enjoined the Bohemian to keep silent at the risk of life and limb, I stepped with him into the circles, whereupon he began to shake like a leaf. Now since I had a spectator I was obliged to make the whole thing believable and to use an incantation in a foreign language, for which reason I did it in Slovenian and said with my eyes rolled upward and with curious gestures: 'Here I stand amidst the signs which fool simpletons and knock the lice off fools' caps; therefore, tell me, you Farter General, where Seyfried with the Horny Skin hid the four sides of pork he stole last night from this fool peasant, so that he might fetch them the following night with the help of his comrades!'

"And after I had repeated this incantation a few times, I performed such strange acrobatic leaps and bounds in my circle, and imitated the sounds of so many different animals that the Bohemian, as he himself later confessed to me, would have shit in his pants if he had not understood my buffoonish incantation. Now as soon as I tired of this, I answered myself in a hollow, muffled voice which sounded as if it were coming from far away: 'The four sides of pork are hidden under the straw in the stall in the outbuilding.' And with that my entire witchcraft was done; the Bohemian could hardly contain his laughter till we stepped outside the circle. 'Oh, my brother!' he said to me in Bohemian, 'you are a fine scoundrel to make fools of people like that!'; but I said to him in the same language: 'And you are indeed a rogue if you do not keep this trick secret till we get out of here, for this is the way to scratch a peasant where he itches.' He promised to keep his mouth shut, and he not only did so, but in fact made up a pack of lies in the bargain about the *spectra* which he had seen during the whole affair, so that people who had only heard me from outside the house believed everything, and bore witness to it with great firmness, so that they took me for an adept in black magic, and both peasants and soldiers henceforth called me 'The Exorcist.'

"And I soon got more requests for that sort of work, and I believe that had I remained with the same regiment much longer, some would have believed me capable of making not only single cavalrymen in the field invisible, but even entire patrols and squadrons. After the peasant got his pork back, he paid me the two sovereigns with profuse thanks, and he wined and dined me and the soldiers quartered with him the whole livelong day.''

CHAPTER 13

By what strokes of fortune Hopalong became once more a musketeer with the Swedish army, then a pikeman with the Imperial army, and finally a freebooter

Simplicius' old mother, who together with his dad had been listening to this tale, now spoke up and said: "Oh, you old shit! Weren't you the peasant-fleecer, the sly chicken-thief!"

"What, mother!" answered Hopalong. "Chicken thief? Don't think I wasted my time on such trifles, on such childish tricks! I stole only four-footed animals, and only healthy ones to boot, or I would not deign to take them. And in fact, old cows were the poorest grade I ever set out to take as booty, and nevertheless in my time I helped rob and steal so many of them that if all them were tied together in a line, tail-to-horn, they would surely reach from here to your farm, despite the fact that your farm, I hear tell, is four Swiss miles[1] from here. Do you really have any idea how many horses, oxen, fatted hogs, and fat sheep I have stolen! Do you really suppose that, what with all these large animals, I had time to think about small ones like chickens, geese, and ducks?"

"Yes, yes!" said Simplicius' mother. "And that is why the dear Lord put an end to your trade and an end to your one leg at the knee, so that from now on you must stand idly by in wartime and leave honest peasants in peace and beg for your daily bread, in punishment for your thieving ways."

At this Hopalong roared with laughter and said: "Be quiet, dear mother! Your son Simplicius did not behave a hair better than I did, and yet he still has both his legs, from which you may deduce that I did not lose my leg because I sinned against the peasantry. Soldiers are born to plague the peasants, and if they don't, they are not doing their duty."

Simplicius' mother answered that the devil in hell would give them their reward, for when a father has sufficiently chastised his child, he is wont to throw the switch into the fire.

"No, mother, you are wrong," said Hopalong, "for as the old proverb or rhyme about good soldiers says:

> As soon as a soldier is born,
> To him three peasants are sworn:
> Number One must see that he's fed,
> Number Two puts a wife in his bed,
> Number Three goes to hell in his stead.

And rightly so, for in the turmoil of the past wars some peasants behaved much worse than the God-fearing soldiers themselves, in that they not only murdered soldiers, guilty or innocent, whenever they could, but also robbed their own neighbors, even their own kith and kin, whenever they had the chance."

Simplicius said: "What good does it do to argue about this? It is the pot calling the kettle black, six of one and half a dozen of the other. The soldiers called the peasants rascals, and the peasants called the soldiers thieves, so that to hear people tell it, there was not a single honest man left in the country. And that is why it is necessary that through the blessed declaration of peace the past was forgiven and forgotten, and everyone's good name restored. But tell us how you fared later, particularly how you came by that heroic name of 'Hopalong.' "

"Courage, that crowbait!" answered Hopalong, "saddled me with that name,[2] and I should have little to say about that witch if the rest of my story did not require it. I fell in with that slut after I had, with a sum of money, bought for her sake my discharge from the aforementioned regiment. But I cannot say whether I was her husband or her servant. I suppose I was both, and her fool to boot, and for that very reason I should rather conceal than make public the things that took place between her and me. But since this toadying scribe of hers has bared them in her fine biography,[3] let anyone who will read them there. I surely have no desire to trumpet my own cuckoldry from the housetops. It is enough for me that I cannot but believe that she spared me as little as yourself. One thing is for sure, my dear Simplice: that at that time her entrancing beauty was of such power that she could have attracted men far better than myself. Indeed, she would have merited the attentions of the most noble and honorable gentlemen, if she had not been so godless and wicked; but she was besotted with the lust for money, so ready, willing, and able to indulge in all sorts of rascality and thievish tricks to get it, and so *insationabilis* in sating her vile carnal lusts, that I am firmly convinced that no one would have committed a sin if he had spared the wood for burning her by putting a millstone around her neck and drowning her without benefit of judge and jury. This monster, when she had grown tired of me,[4] succeeded, both by bribes and, I must admit, also with her doughty fists, on which she relied, in forcing me to quit her, against my own heart's desires. To be sure, she gave me some money, a horse, clothes, and arms to take along with me, but then she also gave me that bottle imp,[5] because of whom I suffered great trepidation till I had safely got rid of him again.

"Now after I had left this *bestia* in this fashion and had gone first to Württemberg under Master General Major von Altringen,[6] then to Thuringia, and finally to Hesse, we there joined forces with other troops. But we did not accomplish anything, but instead melted away again like snow. On patrol I myself was captured by the Swedes,[7] in whose forces I was once more obliged to serve as a musketeer, till the Imperials got their hands on me again[8] not far from Bacharach, but not till after I had helped the Swedes take Würzburg, Wertheim, Aschaffenburg, Mainz, Worms, Mannheim, and several other towns.[9] Then I was sent to Westphalia to serve under the famous von Pappenheim,[10] who was protecting the episcopates of the Prince Elector of Cologne[11] against the Hessians.

"I was forced to carry a pike, which was so repugnant to me that I should rather have let them hang me than fight with such a weapon for any length of time. I did not feel at all like the Swabian lad[12] who gathered to his breast a half-dozen such staffs, for just one of them was eighteen feet too long for me; for which reason I was forever trying to find a way to get rid of it honorably. Now a musketeer, to be sure, is a poor, harried creature, but compared to a miserable pikeman he enjoys lordly good fortune. It is sad to contemplate, much less to tell, of the hardships these poor boobies are obliged to suffer, and you cannot really believe it unless you have been one yourself. And therefore I think that anyone who slays a pikeman when he could spare his life is murdering an innocent man and can never justify such a homicide, for even though these poor dumb cattle (as they are contemptuously called) are assigned the task of protecting brigades against cavalry attack in the open field, they do not, on their own accord, do anyone any harm at all, and anyone who runs into their long spears gets what he deserves. *In summa,* I have seen many hot encounters in my day, but I have seldom seen a pikeman kill anyone.

"We were camped along the Weser River near Hameln when I persuaded my comrade to lend me his musket for a bit of looting and to carry my pike for me till I came back with some booty. I was lucky, for three of us, one of whom was a native of the region and knew every nook and cranny thereabouts, found out about a wagon full of provisions which was going from Bremen to Cassel and had only one lone Hessian musketeer as convoy guard. Because of him, we were obliged to go ahead as far as the Harz Forest, and then when the wagon came to a place which suited us, we attacked and in one salvo shot down the musketeer, the drayman, and his helper, because each of us had taken dead aim at his man. Then we unhitched the six beautiful horses and hastily opened as many bales and barrels as we could, in which containers there was much silkenware and English cloth. But our best find was in a keg full of cards, namely, about 1,200 sovereigns, which as a matter of fact I myself found, but nevertheless divided fairly with my comrades. We pushed the horses almost beyond their limit, and by putting a long distance behind us in a short time, we escaped all danger and returned to our army just as Pappenheim was getting ready to dislodge General Bannier[13] from Magdeburg.

"Now even though Bannier broke camp in disorder and prepared to flee before we could really engage him in battle, he still could not act fast enough to keep from leaving several hundred men from his rear guard on the field. And after we had taken care of everything pretty well, taken the garrison, and pretty well ruined and blown up the walls and bulwarks which fortified that city, or rather that heap of rubble, I got my captain to release me by giving him a pretty good sum of money, which he was all the more willing to do since I did not belong to his unit anyway, but to a regiment of dragoons which was at that time with Tilly's army.

"And so I once more got rid of my vexatious pike, outfitted myself and a servant in the best fashion, and took service with a cavalry regiment as a freebooter, till I might rejoin the regiment to which I really belonged."

CHAPTER 14

Tells of Hopalong's further fortunes and misfortunes

"With this *corpo*[1] I shared in the good fortune of Pappenheim, who after this lucky stroke went through Westphalia like a whirlwind, and that was the life I had always wished for. While he was taxing Lemgo, Herford, Bielefeld, and other cities,[2] I was plundering the villages round about and the peasants in the countryside. When we took Paderborn, however, there was, to be sure, no booty for me, but when we attacked Bannier with his four regiments and trounced Duke George of Lüneburg,[3] good fortune followed in the wake of my customary audacity and brought me all the more plunder. At Stade,[4] where we dislodged the Swedish general, Tott, and acted as we had earlier at Magdeburg, I took prisoner a captain-of-horse and with him a golden chain worth three hundred ducats. Besides that, my servant and I rounded up so many horses that I could have easily passed for a horse trader. And since my money and my good fortune were both increasing, I began to consider whether I ought not to become an officer.[5]

"Everywhere we went we reaped victory and honor, except that we were not able to dislodge the Dutchmen from their entrenchments at Maestricht.[6] We plucked clean the Hessian and Baudis[7] at will, and we taught some fancy steps to the Duke of Lüneburg, who was making an attempt to take Wolffenbüttel, so that he was forced to seek protection[8] under the cannons of the Duke of Brunswick. And, after we had conquered Hildesheim, our General Pappenheim hastened like an anxious bridegroom to join Wallenstein[9] and the forthcoming battle at Lützen, in which, however, the bravest hero on each side and the most famous general of the time was crowned in the midst of his good fortune not with the victory wreath of laurel, but with the burial wreath of myrrh and rue.[10]

"Now after the great Gustavus Adolphus and our renowned Pappenheim, both fighting valiantly, had departed this life at the same time and on the same flank, for it is said that the Count survived the King by barely more than a quarter or half-hour, look you, then the soldiers on both sides really began to fight with raging ferocity. Each side stood firm as a stone wall, and the lifeless bodies of those who had fallen in the *battaglia* formed a waist-high breastwork for their own staunch party. It was as if this battlefield, having been moistened with the martial blood of two such brave heros, had acquired a special strength and power to spur on and incite both the quick and the dead to show how a good soldier is duty-bound to act in that sort of battle; thus both sides perservered with such steadfastness till pitch-black night separated the exhausted surviving remnants of these two valiant armies from each other.

"That same night we fled to Leipzig, and subsequently to Bohemia, despite the fact that our enemy did not have the strength to pursue us, and when I took stock of my own situation, I became aware that I had lost my servant in the battle, and in the baggage train my stable boy and all my possessions. This latter loss, to be sure, our own troops had inflicted on me, and since the same thing happened to many others too, many of those who did the plundering were strung up; but that did not get me back what I had lost.

"This battle and the losses I suffered in it were only the beginning and, as it were, merely an omen of, or *preludium* to, the misfortune which was to continue to plague me for some time to come, for when the Altringer troops recognized me, I was obliged to become once more a dragoon in the same regiment in which I had originally served as one, and in this way not only did my life as a freebooter come to an end, but since I had also lost everything but my clothes, my weapons, and my horse, all hope of becoming an officer was also, as the Czechs say, *pryc*.[11]

"In this condition I helped as an honest soldier to take Memmingen and Kempten[12] and to flay Forbus,[13] the Swedish general, but in all three engagements the only booty I got was the plague, and that, as a matter of fact, just after we had gone to Saxony and Silesia with Wallenstein. Two of us from my company stayed behind with this loathesome disease and faithfully kept each other company in our misery. When I consider the many wretched things which can befall a soldier, it astonishes me that at least some men do not lose all desire to go to war, but it astonishes me even more when I see that old soldiers, who have suffered all manner of misfortune, misery, and want, who have experienced much, and have several times barely escaped their enemy, nevertheless do not quit the war, unless, of course, the war itself comes to an end, or unless they are physically no longer capable of marching and fighting. I do not know what strange, heedless madness possesses us. But I reckon that it is the same sort of folly which afflicts courtiers when they refuse to retire from life at court—which they are always grumbling about—till they fall out of favor with their prince and are obliged to give it up, whether they want to or not.

"We stayed in a small town which was also afflicted with our *contagio;* in fact we stayed with a barber who was as much in need of our money as we were of his medicine, even though each had little of what the other needed, for the barber was poor, and we were not rich, for which reason I was obliged to pay out every day one link of the gold chain which I had snatched at Stade, till we regained our health. And when we dared sit a horse again, we set out through Moravia to Austria, where our regiment was occupying good winter quarters.

"But look you, one misfortune begets another. The two of us, weak and still half sick, were attacked by a band of robbers, who looked to us more like peasants than soldiers, and were forced to dismount, were stripped naked, and were given a bad beating in the bargain. And we were hard put to get away with our lives and to get from them in return for our clothes their old rags, in order to protect ourselves from the winter cold, which was then quite bitter; but these rags did not help much more than if we had dressed in torn fishnets, because it was cold enough to freeze the very blood in your veins. I had had time to swallow several links of my gold chain and put all my faith and trust in them, but I do believe that the devil himself must have told them about that, for they kept us prisoner for two days, till they had recovered all the links from my excrement, and I cannot but consider myself lucky that they did not slice open my belly, but instead finally let us off with our lives. In this wretched condition, lacking money, clothing, weapons, health, and good weather for our journey, we were barely able to move a few people to pity and to come to our aid with a night's lodging and a crust of bread. And it certainly was a good thing for us that I, like my comrade, was not a *niemezy* or *niemey*[14] who did not know Slovenian, since I was able, by parlaying in this language, to beg both food and old clothes from Moravian countrymen, so that even though we were not dressed much more elegantly than before, we were at least better protected against the ferocious winter cold. In this impoverished condition we crept slowly through Moravia, suffering much misery and receiving more pointed and insulting remarks than contributions and alms from the peasants, who never do look with favor on soldiers.''

CHAPTER 15

How heroically Hopalong comported himself in the Battle of Nördlingen

"Upon rejoining our regiment we were outfitted with horses and gear. Wallenstein, however, was murdered at Eger[1] because, it was said, he was about to go over to the opposite side with all his armies, to extirpate the Imperial house of Austria, and to proclaim himself King of Bohemia. By his death, to be sure, the most worthy house of Habsburg was saved, but at the same time the Imperial army, (some of whose officers were suspected of having joined in the accursed Wallenstein conspiracy), was deemed unfit for military use because its loyalty must first be tested, and for this reason we were required to swear once more fealty to the Emperor. But this delay brought it to pass that the Imperial side began to conduct the war in a slovenly fashion, so that here and there the Swedish generals began to attack in force, taking various cities, till finally the most invincible Ferdinand III,[2] then King of Hungary and Bohemia, took up arms himself. He inspected us and led us, sixty thousand strong, together with an incomparable artillery, to Regensburg[3] in Bavaria, which city I had once before helped to take by subterfuge, after I had been obliged to allow Courage to divorce me, and whence I had been sent under the command of my general, Altringer, and with Johann de Werdt,[4] against the Swedes under the command of Gustav Horn.[5] Here then, the fighting got rather hot, particularly on the bridge at Landshut,[6] where I not only had my horse shot from under me, but also—more important for our cause—our aforementioned good General von Altringer was shot dead.

"Now after Regensburg and Donauwörth had fallen into our hands and the Spanish Ferdinand, Cardinal-Infant, with his whole army had joined forces with us, we moved on Ries[7] and laid siege to Nördlingen.[8] At that time I was without a mount, and otherwise too, where money was concerned, a poor devil (since I had not fared well in winter quarters, had suffered illness, and had not taken any booty in a long time), so that no one paid any heed at all to me, or gave me any orders when the Swedes came to relieve the besieged city. But when, because of this, a very bloody battle[9] then ensued, I made up my mind to take some booty too, or else lose my life in the attempt; for I much preferred being dead to being the sort of sluggard who stands idly by and watches, while other honest and well-equipped soldiers contend boldly for the top prize. And since I did not care whether the Emperor or the Swedes won, just as long as I got my share from the fighting, look you, although I had no weapons I mingled with the throng when victory still hung in the balance and the greater part of the armies was still covered with smoke and dust. Just then the Swedish cavalry turned tail and fled the *battaglia,* because they saw that their side had already lost; but when the Lothringian,[10] Johann de Werth, the Hungarians, and the Croats chased them back again across the same field, where I was intent on hurriedly searching and plundering the corpses lying here and there, I was forced to drop to the ground and pretend to be one of the corpses I had intended to rob. This I did several times, till the troops which were chasing each other had passed by, quitting the field and leaving behind the dead and dying, of whom they left a goodly number each time.

"I had hardly gotten to my feet again when a fine-looking and well-equipped officer who was lying there, holding his horse by the bit, with one leg shot to pieces and the other foot still hanging in the stirrup, called to me for help, because he was unable to help himself. 'Alas, brother,' he cried, 'help me!' 'Sure,' I thought to myself: 'Now I am your brother, but a quarter of an hour ago you would not have deigned to say a single word to me, unless it be to call me a dog!' I asked: 'What side are you on?' He answered: 'Good Swedish!' Thereupon I grabbed the horse by the bit and with my free hand snatched one of his own pistols, and with it snuffed out the little bit of pleading life he still had left in him. And this is how that accursed gunpowder has changed warfare, namely, so that a lowly sluggard can take the life of the bravest hero, if said hero has first been damaged a bit by some other wretched stable-rat.[11] I found on him gold coins of a sort which I did not know, because in all my days I had never seen any of such size. His swordbelt was embroidered in gold and silver, his sword hilt was made of silver, and his stallion was an incomparable war-horse such as I had never thrown a leg across in all my days. I took all these things, and when I sensed that it would be dangerous to fart around there with him much longer, or even strip him of his clothes, I mounted the horse, and while reloading the pistols (for his holsters—or gun-cunts, as the peasants call them—were, as was then the custom, well supplied with shells), I could not but sigh and reflect that if even the strong and invincible Hercules were still alive today, he too could be felled by the lowest of stableboys, in the same way as this brave officer had been.

"I rode at full gallop behind our lines and found that there was nothing left to do but to kill, capture prisoners, and take booty, all of which are sure signs of victory. I availed myself of the fruits of others' labors and helped the victors in their work, at which I did not have particularly good luck, 'tis true, for I was hardly able to snap up enough to clothe myself. The other fellows of my regiment had the same ill luck, some more so than others, despite the fact that they had fought bravely."

CHAPTER 16

Where Hopalong tramps around after the Battle of Nördlingen and how he was besieged by some wolves

"Inasmuch as after this mighty and memorable battle the great and victorious Imperial army was sent to various countries, all the provinces where they went felt the effect of the aforementioned bloody encounter, suffering not only the ravages of War, but also those of both Famine and Pestilence. Indeed, they felt how cruelly these three scourges, playing a terrible *harmonia*,[1] can make men dance the dance of death. My own share of the misfortune which those terrible times visited upon almost all of Europe I suffered in the most unfortunate towns of all, namely, those along the Rhine; this, more than all other German rivers, was flooded with sorrow, since it was forced to suffer War, Famine, and Pestilence, and finally all three scourges at one and the same time; in which restless times, which brought many to their eternal rest, or unrest, I once more helped the Emperor take Speyer, Worms, Mainz, and some other towns.[2] Duke Bernhardus of Weimar was then engaged in constant skirmishes against the forces of the French flank of the Rhine, and in his constant maneuvering (for he used the Rhine the way a skillful checkers player does the board), brought ruin not only to the adjoining countries, but also to his own. But when, without any actual swordplay, he most severely despoiled our army in particular, which was at that time under the command of Count Philipp von Mansfeld,[3] look you, I too was ruined. Not only my horse, which I had acquired at Nördlingen (wherever we marched there were dead horses lying about which bore witness to the demise of our army), but also my good money which I had gotten there. For whenever a horse died on me, I bought another one, paying for it with my Spanish reals, English Jacobuses, rose ryals,[4] etc., which I thought to be Spanish and English coins, one of which, to my mind, was worth, and as good as, two or three of the silver ones; and in fact, everyone was happy to take them from me at this rate, as long as I had any of them to spend.

"Now when I had quickly gone through my wealth in this manner, just as the whole country had done with its wealth, the paltry remnants of our once incomparable regiment went to Westphalia, where under Count von Götz[5] we helped take the cities of Dortmund, Paderborn, Hamm, Unna, Kamen, Werl, Soest, and others also.[6] And at that time I was garrisoned in Soest, where, my dear Simplice, you and I became friends and comrades, and since you already know what sort of life I led there, there is no need to tell about it.[7]

"But no more than nine months after you had been taken prisoner by the enemy, and hardly three months after Count von Götz had marched out of Westphalia, Colonel S. Andreas,[8] the commandant of Lippstadt, took Soest by storm. At that time I lost everything I had scraped and scrounged together over a long time. My savings, and I myself, were captured by two fellows from the garrison at Coesfeld,[9] where I was obliged to serve as a musketeer and patiently stay within the garrison walls, till both the Hessians and the French-Weimar troops crossed the Rhine into the Archbishopric of Cologne,[10] where a life began such as I had long sighed for.

"For we found a bountiful country and, under Lampoy,[11] troops so poorly armed that we easily mastered them and dislodged them from their entrenchments at Kempen, putting them to rout, in fact. After this victory came others at Neuss, Kempen, and some other towns, without the good quarters which we had enjoyed earlier, and without the good booty which we had taken now and again. But I, poor booby, did not grow rich from it in the beginning, because I was obliged to remain with my company of musketeers; but after we had looted Jülich and been allowed to do as we pleased with the people in the countryside, as well as with those in both the Archbishopric of Cologne and the Duchy of Jülich, I raked and scraped together enough money to buy my freedom from the company of musketeers and to equip myself once more as a trooper of horse.

"This I did at a time when these towns had already been nearly stripped bare, namely, when we were trying vainly to frighten Lechenich[12] into surrendering, and when not only the Bavarians, who were near Zons,[13] but also the Spanish were after our hides. Because of this threat, Guebriant slipped out of the snare, quitted the Rhine, and led us through the Thuringian Forest to Franconia,[14] where we again found much to rob, plunder, and steal, but no one to fight, till we got into

Württemberg. There, to be sure, Jean de Werth fell upon us at nighttime not far from Schorndorf[15] and got his teeth into us, but without ruffling our fur too badly. But if you are unlucky, you'll bloody your nose even when you fall on your back. For shortly thereafter, while on patrol, I was taken prisoner[16] by Lieutenant-Colonel Bigger, whom the common soldiers were wont to call 'Bugger';[17] and at Hechingen, which was then the Bavarian headquarters, I was put back once more into the same regiment of dragoons in which I had served when I first went to war.

"Thus I once more became a dragoon, but only on foot, because I could not yet afford a horse. We were camped at that time in Balingen, and during that same time a curious thing happened to me which, to be sure, was of no importance, but which was nevertheless so strange and astonishing and afforded me so little pleasure that I must tell about it, even though many who are not acquainted with the wretched state of the ruined German lands of that time will not believe what I say.

"Because our commanding officer in Balingen had received information that the Weimar troops under Reinhold von Rosen[18] had set out with twelve hundred horse to capture us, he decided to report this to all and sundry who might give us succour. Since I, as reported above, still had no mount, and especially since I was well acquainted with all the highways and byways, and also because my reputation was such that they believed that I would carry out the mission successfully, I was sent in peasant garb to Villingen with a written message, reporting the aforementioned *cavalcada* led by von Rosen. And it did not matter whether I were taken prisoner by the enemy on the way or not, for if that happened the enemy would find out that his plan had been discovered and would consequently desist from it. But I got through safely, and toward evening departed again so that I might go back to Balingen before nightfall. Now as I was passing through a village in which there was not a mouse left alive, not to even speak of cats, dogs, and other animals, much less of human beings, I saw a large wolf with its jaws agape advancing *recta* towards me.[19] I was frightened, as you can well imagine, since I had no weapon with me save a stick, and therefore I retreated into the nearest house and should gladly have clapped the door shut behind me if only there had been one, but the house had no doors, or windows, or a stove either. I certainly did not think that the wolf would follow me into the house, but he was so insolent as to show no respect for a place designed for human habitation; instead, he trundled casually along behind me in good wolf fashion, for which reason I was obliged to seek *refugium* up the first flight of stairs, and then the second. And since the wolf let me know that he could climb stairs as well as I could, I was forced to climb in great haste through a skylight and on to the roof, which, to be sure, I was barely able to do, just in the nick of time. Then I was obliged to hastily remove and break the tiles so as to get a foothold on the lattice-work underneath, up which I climbed higher and higher. And when I was high enough and thus safe from the wolf, I opened a larger hole in the roof in order to see if the wolf would go back down the stairs, or whatever else he might do.

"Now when I peered down, look you, he had more of his comrades with him, staring at me and by their gestures acting as if they were about to vote on a plan by which they might get hold of me. I, for my part, bombarded them with half and whole tiles, but the lattice-work made it impossible for me to throw accurately or with all my might and main; and even when I did hit one or the other of them, they paid no attention to it, but instead kept me besieged and blockaded there. In the meantime pitch-black night had fallen which, as long as it covered the horizon, treated me most unkindly, with sharp cutting winds and occasional snow flurries, for it was the beginning of November and therefore fairly cold weather, so that I fared miserably on the roof on this long winter's night. To make matters even worse, after midnight the wolves began to make such horrifying music that I thought their gruesome howling could not but make me tumble off the roof.

"*In summa,* it is impossible to imagine what a miserable night I spent. And just because of the extreme danger in which I found myself, I began to ponder on the miserable state of the inconsolable, damned souls in hell, who must suffer throughout eternity and who are tormented not merely by a few wolves but by terrible devils, who are trapped not merely on a roof but in hell itself, who must suffer not merely cold but eternally burning fire, and who must suffer not for one night, with the hope of being rescued, but forever and ever. This night seemed to me four times longer than any other in my life, so that I began to fear that dawn would never come, for I heard neither clocks striking nor cocks crowing, and on this hard roof I sat so frozen in the raw wind that towards daybreak I thought I might fall to the ground below at any moment."

CHAPTER 17

Hopalong receives succor and once more becomes a rich dragoon

"On this roof I did live to see the welcome light of day once more, even though I did not see anything from which I might have garnered any hope for my salvation; rather, I had every reason to despair, for I was tired, faint, sleepy, and, on top of that, hungry. I made every effort to keep from falling asleep, because the slightest nod would have been for me the beginning of eternal sleep, since I should then either freeze to death or tumble down off the roof. In the meantime, the wolves continued to stand guard over me, even though occasionally a few of them wandered up and down the stairs. At those who stayed in the house up under the roof I kept throwing tiles in hopes that I might drive them off; it did me no good, however, except that this *exercitium* kept me awake and put some vestige or a *copei* of warmth into my bones. And I spent almost the whole day in this way.

"Towards evening, however, when I was already almost resigned to a horrible death, there came quietly cantering along five fellows, and I could tell straightway from the fact that they were carrying their arms at the ready that they were reconnoitering the village. I recognized the last rider by his horse to be a sergeant in Colonel Sporck's regiment[1] who knew me well. The riders in front saw me from a distance and at first took me to be a sentry and, when they got closer, to be a peasant, and they therefore commanded me, as they would a peasant, to climb down or be shot down. But I called the aforementioned sergeant by name and thereby identified myself, and I assured them besides that in the last twenty-four hours not a living soul had been in the village, since I had been standing guard on the roof for that long; at the same time I straightway told them what my business was and what manner of creatures were keeping me under this onerous arrest. Hereupon Colonel Sporck himself straightway arrived with a large band of troops. When he heard of my plight, he straightway had ten cavalrymen with their carbines dismount, some to go into the house and others to surround it;

and he also had guards posted outside the village. Now when these men stormed the house eight wolves were shot or otherwise killed, and in the cellar were found five corpses, of which the wolves had even chewed up some of the bones. Upon finding a knife, a flint, two passes, and a letter of exchange drafted on Ulm, as well as a belt with ducats sewn in it, it was established that one of the corpses was that of a butcher who had been travelling down the Danube to buy some Hungarian oxen. And besides the remains of these five human beings, we also found the carcasses of other animals, so that this cellar looked like a knacker's yard.

"The aforementioned colonel was on a mission with five hundred horse to reconnoiter Rottweil and to find out what the Duke of Weimar's troops were planning, and when he learned from me what von Rosen's intentions were, he straightway ordered the horses to be fed in this same village, that is, to give the horses some of the feed which each trooper was carrying with him, for in the village there was nothing for the horses to eat but the thatch on some of the roofs. And then everyone also fed himself, and I was generously given some of the colonel's cold viands, of which at that time I certainly had great need.

"The colonel took the encounter with the wolves to be a good omen that they would find yet more unexpected booty. He planned to proceed to Balingen and, together with our own dragoons who were camped there, to deal a blow to von Rosen. I was put on a spare horse to show them the most direct route, but before we had marched even two hours into the night, we received information that von Rosen had indeed been seen at Balingen, but not with the intent of dislodging the dragoons, but of occupying the town, which he had thought to be empty. But because he arrived too late, he had stopped in the village of Geislingen to spend the night there. Hereupon our colonel straightway changed his plan of attack and marched straight to Geislingen, where we arrived unexpectedly at eleven o'clock and most rudely awakened von Rosen and the four regiments with him from their sleep. Nearly three hundred cavalrymen entered the village, while others stayed outside it and set fire to it on all sides; then, in an instant, it seemed, these four regiments were routed and destroyed. Two hundred men, not counting the officers, were taken prisoner, and much fine booty was taken too. And since I had been given permission by the colonel to go into the village to look for booty, I crept through the houses at the edge of the village closest to a place which was burning and captured three handsome horses under saddle, with full gear, and a page whose master, along with his servant, has either fled on foot or had hidden himself somewhere because he feared the bullets of our cavalry outside the village, who generally attacked only those who were fleeing on horseback.

"Early the next morning the colonel allowed me to ride back to Balingen with my booty, to bring to our commanding officer and his dragoons the report of the successfully executed attack on the village. I was welcomed, not only because of the report which I had brought, but also because of the good letter of commendation which the colonel had given me because of my staunch behavior and the risks I had run. My commanding officer had promised me a dozen sovereigns upon my return if I successfully delivered the message, but since I now returned in such good condition, he made me a gift of two dozen of them and on top of that promoted me to corporal. For that reason I turned one of the horses into silver and with that money equipped myself and a servant all the more splendidly, and I also entertained high hopes that in time I might yet play the role of a great man. On the very same day on which I rose so high, Rottweil[2] fell to Guebriant, but the Duke of Weimar's troops did not hold the town much beyond the time of the Tuttlingen Fair,[3] on which occasion I indeed was able to scrounge together but little booty, because as a non-commissioned officer I had other things to do. After this, our General von Mercy[4] retook Rottweil *per accord.*[5] And because at that time I stole some things from the baggage train as it was leaving, I should surely have been stood up before a firing squad (as happened to a number of pilferers) or even hanged (because as a corporal I was supposed to be preventing others from doing just this), if my good horse had not carried me out of danger in good time, and if ten sovereigns which I scattered in front of my pursuers had not saved me from the hands of the provost and hangman.

"Right after this, we were lodged in good winter quarters. And although Corporal Hopalong at first suffered a severe scalp disease, with the result that he did not have a single blade of grass left on his upper meadow, afterwards he fared so well that in the middle of the war his face was as fat as a village mayor's in peacetime."

CHAPTER 18

How Hopalong fared from the Tuttlingen Fair
till after the engagement at Herbsthausen

"The following summer clever General Baron von Mercy once more led us into the field in fine fashion, almost in an Old Franconian or Dutch manner, where everything proceeds in good order. The most outstanding thing, which we accomplished right away, was to seize the town of Überlingen,[1] the garrison of which had for a time now been causing great trouble on and around Lake Constance. After this we took Freiburg[2] in the Breisgau, which for several years in succession had ruled like an Amazon queen over the whole of the Black Forest, levying taxes and enriching herself. We hardly had the city in our power, however, when Duc d'Enghien[3] and Turenne[4] arrived before our well fortified camp to rap our knuckles by storming our bulwarks[5] and sparing neither their soldiers' blood nor lives, as if soldiers just sprout overnight like mushrooms. Like resolute heroes they attacked us with unbelievable fury, but each time they were greeted and repulsed, on horse and on foot, in such fashion that so many of them fell on the battlefield that it looked as if it had snowed soldiers; and it was fitting indeed that those whose lives were thought to be worth nothing should lose their lives for nothing. The next day the battle raged even more fiercely, and I swear that in all my days I have never been in combat where men fought more ferociously than right there at Freiburg! It looked as if the French would or could not bear to leave us undefeated, and for just this reason they fought all the more bravely, in fact foolhardily. We, for our part, fought sensibly and at great advantage. Thus it came about that on our side not many more than a thousand men were killed or wounded, while on theirs more than six thousand were.

"We dragoons, along with the cuirassiers[6] under Jean de Werdt's leadership, did the best, and if there had been more of us on horseback, the French would have paid dearly for their impudence. Of course, we too left the field battered and bruised, but also with great honor, because we had so gallantly withstood such a strong foe and had destroyed a third as many of his men as we ourselves numbered. On the other hand, the French did not suffer any disgrace either, since they displayed sufficiently their rash valor, unless they be criticized or rebuked for needlessly wasting the blood of so many soldiers, or otherwise needlessly butting their heads against a stone wall.

"Now after we had caught our breath again a bit in Württemberg, and while on the march looking about for a bit of plunder, we assumed that we might find it in the Lower Palatinate, for which reason we invaded it and right afterwards took Mannheim[7] by storm, where I once more took considerable booty in the form of money, clothes, and horses, because I was one of the first to enter the city. After this we cleared Höchst[8] of its Hessian garrison *per accord* and took Bensheim[9] by storm, at which place a bullet ended my colonel's life. Here we wreaked havoc more severely than the Bavarians are wont to do and thereby caused Weinheim to surrender to us unconditionally.[10]

"At this time, our army was very well off, for in Mercy we had an intelligent and brave general, and in von Holtz something akin to an Atlas, who knew all about every highway and byway, pass, mountain, river, forest, field, and valley throughout all Germany, so that he was able to both lead and lodge the army most advantageously, and when fighting was about to begin he was able to see quickly what was to his advantage. In Jean de Werdt we had a brave cavalryman in the field with whom the soldiers would rather have gone into battle than into poor winter quarters, because he had the reputation of being very lucky, both in pitched battles and in surprise attacks. In Württemberg and the neighboring lands we had a good breadbasket which seemed to have been created expressly for our sustenance and to provide us with winter quarters. The Prince Elector of Bavaria[11] himself, truly an experienced general and wise military leader, was, so to say, our father and provider who watched us from afar and directed and led us from his residence with his clever and cautious quill. And, most important of all, we had bold and experienced commanders, both on horse and on foot, and from them down to the last soldier we had trained, tried, and true fighting men. And I might make so bold as to say: If a potentate had an army like this one gathered together at the beginning of a war, he would easily vanquish his opponent, even if the latter had twice as many *tirones*.[12]

"But now I must get back to my story. To put it briefly, it goes like this: After winter quarters most of us went to join the Imperial army in

Bohemia and were dealt our share of blows by the Swedes at Jankau,[13] and they often took out on us their past misfortunes and used us to wipe clean the stains on their escutcheon which they had acquired I know not where or how. In fact, we were often obliged to risk our lives, yes even lose them, which did indeed occur on this occasion too.

"I did not take part in the aforementioned engagement, but was in Württemberg, where at Nagold[14] my commanding officer stupidly ignored his advantage and as recompense for his lack of caution lost his life in a miserable fashion. And at this time it came about that I was promoted from corporal to quartermaster sergeant, just as von Mercy was reassembling our troops from here and there, in order to prevent Turenne from making himself too much at home and too cozy in our province, in Swabia and Franconia, from which we were wont to sustain ourselves.

"And this time von Mercy succeeded by launching a surprise attack against the French at Herbsthausen[15] and thrashing them in such fashion that Turenne was obliged to quit the field, leaving behind many high-ranking officers and generals. Early in this encounter I was shot through the thigh, but not dangerously wounded; nevertheless I was made unfit by this to take booty, for I could not help fight those who were standing firm, nor could I pursue those who were fleeing. This caused me such gripes that I cursed for two solid days without pausing long enough to say a single *pater noster*. For because till now my tough hide had made light of the bullets coming at me, I did not think that anyone could do more than I could, much less do me any harm just when there was booty to be taken.''

CHAPTER 19

Hopalong's further historia up to the Bavarian armistitium

"The fruits of this noteworthy victory, not counting the booty and prisoners taken, were simply this: our army went as far as the border of Lower Hesse and succoured the garrison at Amöneburg,[1] struggled in vain at Kirchhain,[2] and in so doing stirred up a hornet's nest; that is, we caused Turenne to join forces with the Hessians, for which reason we were then obliged to retreat along the same route by which we had advanced. At that time I was in the Tauber River valley along with the other wounded and was having my wounds cured, but when our army, with reinforcements of about 4,500 men brought up by Count von Geleen,[3] moved to Heilbronn and reinforced the garrison of that city with troops under the command of Colonel Fugger, Colonel Caspar, and my colonel,[4] I was obliged to stay there too.

"In the meantime the combined troops of the Hessians, of Turenne, and of Königsmarck marched into the Lower Palatinate, added the army of Duc d'Enghien, and marched up the Neckar River to reach us and our army. To be sure, they did leave us alone in Heilbronn, but Wimpfen[5] fell to them right away when they bombarded it and took it by storm, capturing or killing six hundred of our men there. There they crossed the Neckar and advanced to the Tauber, seizing many undefended towns and also the city of Rothenburg.[6] Finally they forced our army to stand and fight, and won a bloody victory over us at Allersheim,[7] at which town our brave general, Field Marshal von Mercy, also lost his life. Following this they took Nördlingen per accord and forced the major of my regiment, who was in Dinkelsbühl[8] with four hundred of our dragoons and two hundred musketeers, to surrender unconditionally rather than per accord. And because these troops were required to swear allegiance to their captors and serve in their army, our regiment was weakened more than if it had been in the battle itself. From there they hastened through Schwäbisch-Hall to attack us, because they were after us too, and they began to maneuver against us and to dig entrenchments. But as soon as they noted the arrival of our troops, reinforced with sixteen Imperial regiments which Archduke Leopold Wilhelm[9] commanded, look you, they vanished like quicksilver, or at least scattered as if they had never won the battle at Allersheim. And I really cannot see what they gained by this costly *victori*, save that they weakened our side somewhat and got rid of the famous General von Mercy, for they were pursued to Philippsburg and lost all the towns they had conquered before; at Wimpfen we also took from them eight fine demi-cannons, a field piece, a fire-mortar, and there and elsewhere many of their troops, of which all the Germans were required to swear allegiance to our army, which was thus once more strengthened accordingly.[10] Following this, we went back to winter quarters in our usual province, that is, Franconia, in Ansbach and Württemberg, while the Imperial army wintered in Bohemia.

"Before the year ran out, the core of our army marched to Bohemia to join the Imperial troops, in the hope of dealing a good blow to the Swedes, who were also there, but because it was not the right season, and very bad weather to boot, and especially since the Swedes quit this same kingdom of their own accord, nothing came of it, save that several towns held by the Swedes fell into Imperial hands again.

"The following summer,[11] however, when the enemy began to launch attacks between the principalities of Upper and Lower Hesse, we took the field against them in earnest, and marched through the Wetterau[12] to Kirchhain and Amöneburg to do battle with them, where, to be sure, no major engagement took place, but a merry little martial *exercitium*[13] was carried out by regular troops at the Ohm River, during which I took prisoner a Hessian lieutenant and acquired from him a good horse, together with sixty sovereigns in cash. Then we withdrew into the Wetterau, because the enemy did not want to fight, but instead remained in his barricaded and well-provisioned camp not far from Kirchhain, while we were suffering from lack of forage. The Swedes and the Hessians pursued us, after they had joined forces with Turenne. There, one army was drawn up for battle on one side of the Nidda River, the other army on the other side, and they exchanged cannon fire and looked at each other like two snarling dogs, neither of whom dares attack the other unless he has the advantage. Finally they allowed us to march toward the Kamberg Bottom, but they jumped the Main and the Danube and left us eating their dust.

"Our commanding officer,[14] together with Jung-Kolb[15] and his regiment, was sent to steal a march on the combined armies and to fortify one or the other of our own towns. And even though Königsmarck mauled us at Schwabenhausen,[16] we nevertheless arrived at Augsburg still eight hundred horse strong, just as the Swedes were entertaining the vain hope of taking that city without a struggle. Immediately after that we were joined by Colonel Rouyer[17] with 450 dragoons, whereupon the Swedes hurriedly laid siege to us and in a short time dug trenches right up to our gun emplacements; and I do believe that they would have made it mighty hot for us, and would have even conquered the city, if our side had not quickly taken up its position before it; and since we were now strengthened by fresh reinforcements we frightened off the enemy all the more boldly.

"I was obliged to remain with other dragoons on detached duty in this city till Bavaria and Cologne made a sort of half-way peace,[18] or at least (I do not really know what it was) an armistice with the French, Swedes, and Hessians. When this was concluded, I and others too were relieved by footsoldiers, and I returned to my regiment as it was lying around slothfully in the vicinity of Deggendorf.[19]

"But several of our generals and commanding officers[20] could not tolerate such inactivity, and so they made so bold as to go over to the Imperial side with the troops under their command, after first having plundered, however, the lands of their own commander-in-chief, for which they had heretofore so gallantly fought, and among them was my own colonel, who was but a soldier of fortune himself, and who had been promoted to his rank by the grace and generosity of his great Prince Elector;[21] but he did not gain anything by it, save that he had bestowed upon him the infamous title[22] which was here and there posted on gallows' trees in Bavaria; one such monument I myself have seen at St. Nicolao near Passau. Others were forgiven their misbehavior because of their great merit and high esteem, and really did deserve better because of their loyalty and bravery. Now after this uproar had quieted down again, I know of nothing noteworthy to say about myself, unless it be that I went spooning and courting the Bavarian lasses till we once more took up the sword."

CHAPTER 20

Continuation of this historia *up to the conclusion of peace and final mustering out*

"But when our old war started up again, our lucky old stars refused to shine down on us benevolently, as they had before. Mercy was dead, Jean de Werdt was no longer on our side, and Holzapfel, who was also called Melander,[1] was not so fierce and quick against the Swedes and French as he had been against the Imperial troops when he was still serving with the Hessians, even though this honest soldier did his best, and in fact even gave up his life when the enemy chased us across the Lech and the Isar. At that time several of the enemy yelled across the water to us (while we were, in fact, standing firm as a stone wall and could not be budged an inch by the enemy's guns) that we should make haste to take flight, or they would chase us to a place where a cow could be bought for a half-penny. They guessed right when they made that prophecy, and when we were forced by the press of their numbers to follow their advice, I did finally learn that among our troops a cow was sold not only for a half-penny but even for a miserable pipe of tobacco. At that time our situation was wretched: von Gronsfeld[2] was no more able than Melander to have any of our side crowned with laurel wreaths; but rather, those of us who were not in fortified towns were forced to cross the Inn River, which the enemy also made so bold as to do.

"But in this torrential river the torrential course of victory and good fortune of the Swedes and the French came to an end. I was stationed with seven undermanned regiments in Wasserburg[3] when both the French and the Swedish armies attempted to subjugate it and to cross the aforementioned river into the fruitful lands of the other side, in which some people who were as old as the hills had never in all their days even laid eyes on a soldier. But since our brave defense made it impossible for them to accomplish anything here, in spite of the fact that they treated us to red-hot cannon balls, they went to Mühldorf,[4] meaning to do there what they had not been able to do at Wasserburg. But there an Imperial general, one of the von Hunoltsteins,[5] resisted them till they tired of their bootless task and established their main garrison at Pfarrkirchen,[6] where they were first visited by hunger and finally by pestilence, which also in the end would have driven them out between the Tyrolean Alps and the Danube, between the Inn and the Isar, if the general *armistitium,* which preceded the permanent peace, had not allowed them to occupy better quarters.

"During the armistice our regiment was quartered around Hilpold-stein, Heideck, and such places,[7] at which time an amusing prank was played in our regiment. There was a corporal who wanted to be a colonel[8]—I know not what madness drove him to it. A regimental clerk just out of school was his *secretarius,* and others of his toadies also had other *officia* and posts. Many were inclined to follow him, particularly young and inexperienced men, and they either chased the highest rank-ing officers out of camp or otherwise usurped their commands and rightful powers; they allowed noncommissioned officers of my stripe, being neutral, to move about freely in their quarters. And they might have really accomplished great things if they had carried out their plot at another time, namely, in the peril of war, when the enemy was near at hand and we were needed, for our regiment was at that time one of the strongest and consisted of highly trained and well-equipped soldiers who were either old and experienced or young daredevils who had been bred, as it were, in the war. When this fellow, despite well-meant advice, refused to desist from his folly, Lapier and Colonel Elter came with troops under their command and brought the situation at Hilpold-stein under control with no effort and bloodshed; they had the new colonel drawn and quartered, or, more precisely, quinted (for his head also came off), and displayed on wheels at the four roads leading into town. They had eighteen notorious fellows from among his principal followers either beheaded or hanged by their fine necks. They took the muskets away from the regiment and required all of us to swear al-legiance again to our supreme commander. Thus, shortly before my service ended, and before the final peace, I was changed from a quar-termaster sergeant into a quartermaster, and the regiment from dragoons into troopers of horse. And, my dear Simplice, this is all I can tell you about my life during the war in Germany, except that shortly thereafter we were mustered out, at which time I had three good horses, a servant, and a page, about three hundred ducats in cash, not counting the three months' pay which I received when I was discharged. For I had not had any misfortune for some time, but instead had been accumulating money. And thus I was obliged to give up soldiering at the very time when I thought I knew how to do it best. I paid off the servant and the page as best I could, turned two of my horses and everything else of value into silver, and betook myself with this to Regensburg to see how I should proceed further or what manner of fortune might be in store for me.''

CHAPTER 21

Hopalong gets married, plays the role of an innkeeper, which trade he abuses; becomes a widower, and takes French leave

"I was at that time a man of about fifty, and in the aforementioned Regensburg I met a lieutenant's widow who was not much younger and also did not have less money than myself, and since we had seen each other repeatedly in the army, we became good friends all the more quickly. She saw that I had money, and I that she did too, and soon we were teasing each other about whether the two of us might not make a couple; and also we both said that anyone who did not believe it need only figure it out himself. She was a native of that country where all sorts of confessions are permitted,[1] and that was fine with me, because I did not yet adhere to any confession, and thus I could have the choice of going into whichever one of the many I liked best. She was always boasting about how wealthy her family was, and always lamenting that in her youth, right at the beginning of the war, she had been carried off by her late husband, and that he had made her his wife against her will when her homeland had been conquered, from which it was not difficult to tell that she was no longer young, because she was able to remember the first capture of the fortress at Frankenthal[2] as well as I could. But why make a big fuss about it? We both made short shrift of it and quickly got together, not only concerning the marriage contract, but also about the wedding ceremony. In respect to the money and property which each of us brought to the marriage, we agreed and formally contracted, among other things, that if she should die before me and without issue from this marriage (of which there was no hope in her case anyway), then I should have for the rest of my life tenure and use of her farm, but should provide a decent endowment for her son, whom she had had by her first husband. I kept for myself one hundred guilders to bequeath and bestow as I saw fit. Now after the bell had been cast in this fashion, we hurried to her fatherland where I did indeed find a well situated inn, built of stone like a castle, but neither stoves, doors,

81

shutters, nor windows, so that I was obliged to do almost as much building as if I were starting from the ground up. I got all this done with admirable patience, and to good purpose used my own small capital and what my wife had, so that I could be taken to be a fine innkeeper in a fine inn.³ And my wife was able to act the Jew as well as any sixty-year-old native of Jerusalem,⁴ so that our money bag, in spite of the heavy expenses (for I was obliged to pay a peace tax,⁵ although I should have much preferred the war to last longer), became much heavier rather than lighter, primarily because at that time there were many people traveling, both merchants and refugees, and mustered-out soldiers trying to get home, all of whom my wife was able to fleece right skillfully, because her house was well situated for this purpose.

"On the side I also traded horses, which was quite profitable for me, and since my wife was the living example of a skinflint, she also little by little got me in the habit of imitating her and putting all my thought and all my mind to scraping together money and property. And in time I should have become a rich man indeed, if misfortune had not steered me in a different direction.

"Generally, people envy and are hostile to those who prosper, and all the more so if avarice is observed in those who are growing rich. By contrast, generosity generally earns favor, particularly if it is accompanied by humility. This envy I did not perceive till its effects were already being felt; for as soon as my neighbors saw that my riches were visibly flourishing and growing, each of them began to ponder by what means this should happen so frequently to me, so that some of them were even so impudent as to claim that my wife and I were able to practice witchcraft. And so, without my knowing it, everyone was surreptitiously watching exactly what I did and did not do. There was among them in that same town an arch-scoundrel from whom I had earlier bought for a song a nice, large parcel of well-situated and very lovely meadowland, which he begrudged me, even though I had paid him in cash for it. This man conferred with a Dutchman and a Swiss —for people of all different nationalities lived there together—to figure out how they might discover the source of my riches and do me damage. And in this they were all the more diligent because several of their countrymen, because they were not able to adapt to the way of life in this country, had already wasted their money and come to grief. Once I received two wagons full of wine, from which the tax collector had already drawn his share and which had straightway been put into my cellar, as I was to entertain a large wedding party on the following day. Now since these aforementioned three envious fellows thought me capable of turning water into wine, they dumped into my well that very same evening some chopped straw, such as is usually mixed with oats and fed to horses, and when the next day the straw was also found in my wine, look you, I was caught red-handed. All the barrels were examined, and more wine was found than I had laid in, and in every barrel there was some chopped straw, and even though I could swear that I knew nothing of this adulteration, for my wife and her son had been busy this time without me, that did not help me any, for the wine was confiscated, and in addition I was fined a thousand florins. This event my good wife so took to heart that she fell ill out of shame and grief and went the way of all flesh. And they would have even ordered me to close the inn if there had been another such stately edifice in town which would have been suitable for an inn.

"Only after this affair did I realize what kind of friends and foes I had had heretofore. I was held in such contempt that no honest man wanted to have anything to do with me. No one even said 'Hello!' to me anymore, and when I wished someone a good day, they did not even say 'Thank you.' I had no more guests in my inn at all, except for strangers who might perchance stray into it, or people who as yet knew nothing of my reputation. All this I found hard to bear, and because, on top of this, I had dallied with two maidservants, and because the results of this dalliance would soon be there for all to see, I packed up my money and what valuables I could carry, got on my best horse, and, after making it known that, as was my wont, I had business to conduct in Frankfurt, I took the road in the opposite direction, towards the Danube, in order to seek service under Count von Serini,[6] whose brave exploits in the war against the Turks were at that time on everyone's lips.''

CHAPTER 22

*Hopalong's Turkish war in Hungary
and his marriage to
a hurdy-gurdy girl*

"I found and received what I wanted, not in the service of Serini, but in that of the Roman Emperor himself. I arrived at the very same time as several French volunteers[1] who wished to please their king by winning honor against the Turkish saber. I did not like that war by half, and did not even have halfway good luck in it, because right from the start I was baffled by this war, and was not able to find the secret of becoming rich and famous. But I went along with it as well as I could, and in the sharpest engagements I always sought either death or honor and booty, but I never succeeded better than middling fair, and even though sometimes I took some booty, nevertheless I had neither the good fortune, nor the wit, nor the occasion to save and preserve it to my advantage. And in this way, with this sort of booty, I got by till the very last full-scale battle,[2] in which our side, to be sure, came out on top, while I ended up on the bottom, for when my horse was shot, I, though perfectly sound, was pinned under it and was obliged to lie there while both friend and foe rode back and forth several times right over me. I was so miserably trampled by the horses that I fainted and was taken for dead even by the victors, and as a dead man, like the other dead men, robbed of my clothes, into which I had sewn some fine ducats.

"Now when I came to my senses again, I felt exactly as if I had been broken on the wheel, or as if my arms and legs had been beaten to a pulp some other way. I had nothing on save my shirt, and could neither walk, sit, nor stand, and since everyone was bent on robbing the dead and on taking booty, everyone left me lying there till I was finally found by one of my own regiment, through whose good offices I was carried to our baggage train, where one soldier or the other gave me bits and pieces of clothing, and where I was put into the care of a surgeon, who smeared me now and then with his *oleum populeum*.[3]

"Thus I had now become the most miserable wretch in the world. Both the sutler who was supposed to cart me and the surgeon who was supposed to cure me were unwilling to do so, and moreover, I was obliged to suffer from hunger for a measly penny, for they often forgot to give me my rations, and I lacked the strength to go begging. Now when I had in fact resigned myself to the idea that I must finally croak in the sutler's cart, a little bit of good fortune smiled on me once more, in that I was sent to Styria together with other sick and wounded, whither we were removed in order to regain our health. That lasted till some of us were mustered out after the unexpected conclusion of peace,[4] among which persons was myself; and after I had paid my debts, I had neither pence nor farthing left, nor any decent clothes on my back.

"In addition to this, my health was not quite restored yet either. *In summa,* I was at my wit's end, and for me begging was the best trade in which I could engage. It was more profitable for me than the Hungarian war had been, for I found an easy life and sweet sustenance, through which I soon regained my former strength, because people who thought I had fallen into poverty and ill health defending the Bastion of Christendom[5] against the Turks were glad to give me alms.

"Now when I had regained my health completely, it still did not enter my mind to quit my newly adopted way of life and to earn my daily bread in an honorable way; instead, I became good friends and comrades with all kinds of beggars and runagates, especially with a blind man who had many infirm and crippled children,[6] and yet among them one single healthy, straight-limbed daughter who played the hurdy-gurdy and not only earned her daily bread that way, but even put money aside and shared it with her father. Conceited old ass that I was,[7] I fell in love with her, for I thought to myself: 'In your chosen profession she will be a staff to you in your present and now homeless old age.' And so that I might win her love in return and make her my wife, I got a treble violin, to please her, and accompanied her when she played on her hurdy-gurdy on doorsteps and in marketplaces, at peasant dances and country fairs, which brought us quite a bit of money, and what we earned together this way I shared with her even-steven; I let her have the whitest pieces of bread, and whatever food we were given—bacon, eggs, meat, butter, and the like—I turned over completely to her parents, in return for which I occasionally cadged a warm meal from them, especially when I had somewhere or other snatched from a peasant a hen, which her old mother knew how to pluck, stuff, garnish, and prepare, either fried or roasted in good beggar fashion (which is the best possible way). In this way I won the favor of both the old woman and the young one. Indeed, they became so friendly with me that I could no longer conceal or postpone my intentions, but instead asked for the girl's hand in marriage; whereupon I straightway received her father's consent, but with the express condition and proviso that as long as I was married to his daughter I was not to settle down anywhere, nor to abandon the free life of beggars, nor to let anyone induce me into taking service with any master, thereby becoming an honest burgher. Secondly, I was henceforth to give up all thoughts of soldiering. And, thirdly, whenever the blind man commanded, I was to move from one good, peaceful country to another, together with his *familia*. In return for such obedience on my part he promised to guide and lead me in such a way that his daughter and I should suffer no want, even though we might now and again be obliged to make do in a cold barn.

"Our wedding was celebrated at a fair where all kinds of runagates of our acquaintance came together, such as puppeteers, acrobats, sleight-of-hand artists, ballad singers, pin pedlars, scissors' grinders, tinkers, hurdy-gurdy girls, master beggars, rogues, and other honorable rabble of that stripe. A single old barn was enough to serve as banquet hall and bridal chamber. Here we sat around on the ground like Turks, but we drank like good Germans. The groom and his bride were obliged to make do with straw for a bed, because more reputable guests had taken over all the inns, and when the groom began to grumble because the bride had not brought her maidenhead intact, she said: 'Are you such a miserable fool that you expect to find in a hurdy-gurdy girl what better fellows than you do not find in their allegedly chaste brides? If that is what you are thinking, then I'll laugh myself sick at your simplemindedness and stupidity, particularly since that is the reason why you were not required to give me a morning gift.'⁸ What was I to do? The damage had been done. To be sure, I began to look somewhat down in the mouth, but she told me in so many words that if I was inclined to despise her because of such foolishness, which was a mere figment of the imagination anyway, then she knew other fellows who would not disdain her company.''

CHAPTER 23

Hopalong gets rid of his blind father-in-law,
his mother-in-law, and his wife,
one after the other

"Even though for a long time afterwards I had very cranky crotchets in my *capitolio* because of this hoax, my hurdy-gurdy girl was nevertheless so cunning, crafty and friendly that little by little she dispelled these thoughts, for she said that if it meant that much to me, she would gladly grant me, even herself make arrangements for me to take, by rape as it were, the maidenhead of some other girl. But the young crowbait was exaggerating and kept such a tight rein on me that I forgot all about other women; and it was she who taught me not to buy for any woman even a piece of cloth, even if it were on sale every day. She finally got me to the point where I was almost the servant, and she and her parents my masters, in spite of the fact that I brought in so much with my fiddle, sleight-of-hand tricks, and other entertainment that I might have had a full trough and idle days without them. On top of that, I was not a little plagued by jealousy, because I was often obliged to observe with my own two eyes that she behaved much more wantonly and lewdly with other fellows than behooved a pious hurdy-gurdy girl. That I suffered all this, however, and finally even resigned myself to it completely, was because I did not trust my own age, worrying that its approaching frailty might throw me into an illness during which I should then be forsaken by all the world if I offended this reputable wife of mine and her honorable kinfolk, who, as I alone knew, had nearly three hundred sovereigns in cash to use for just such an emergency. And what is more, I finally gave my wife free rein to do whatever pleased the wanton young thing, because I myself did not desire much any more. For my part, I passed the idle days eating and drinking. Finally I became so inured to this vagabond life which we led very cozily with one another that in the end I paid no more heed to respectability.

"In the meanwhile we tramped through Lower and Upper Austria, the strip of land along the Enns, the Archbishopric of Salzburg, and a good part of Bavaria, where my father-in-law died of apoplexy, the mother soon following after him and leaving us to take care of five miserable cripples. The oldest son wanted to be his own master and seek alms on his own, and my wife and I were quite willing to let him do it. For each of the remaining four, there were twenty masters who wanted them, all of them fat beggarwomen, who took on such creatures to use their misery to arouse sympathy, in order to collect alms. We gladly let them go with these masters, because we were determined to earn our daily bread no longer by playing the role of miserable beggars, but by playing instead our musical instruments, which seemed to be more reputable and, I think, better suited to my wife.

"For this reason I had her and myself outfitted in a little better clothing, namely, in the fashion in which hurdy-gurdy folk are wont to appear. Also, in addition to my bag of tricks I acquired some puppets, with which I now and then amused the peasants for money, for we set out and followed the annual country and religious fairs,[1] which little by little increased our money considerably. One day we were sitting side by side in the shade on the lovely bank of a gently flowing stream, not only to rest our bones, but also to eat and drink what we were carrying with us. We were making plans on how we were going to combine the puppet show with a lottery, a roulette wheel, a dice table and a strap game[2] in order to increase our profits with them, for we thought that if one of them did not work, the other one would. While we were talking I saw something on the water in the shadow or reflection of a tree which was lying in the fork of a branch but which nevertheless I could not see in the tree itself;[3] this I pointed out to my wife because it was so strange. After she had looked at it and marked the fork where it lay, she climbed up the tree and fetched down what we had seen reflected in the water. While watching her I became aware that she disappeared the exact instant at which she picked up in her hand the thing whose shadow we had seen reflected in the water, yet I still saw her form clearly reflected in the water as she was climbing back down the tree, holding in her hand a little bird's nest which she had taken out of the tree. I asked her what kind of a bird's nest she had there, whereupon she asked me whether I could really see her. I answered: 'In the tree itself I do not see you, but your reflection in the water I do see.' 'That is good,' said she. 'When I come down you'll see what I have.' It seemed very strange to me that I should hear my wife speaking and yet not see her, and even stranger that

I saw her shadow walking in the sun, but not her herself! And when she came nearer to me and into the shade so that she herself no longer threw a shadow because she was now out of the sunshine and in the shade, I could see nothing more of her at all, except that I heard the little noises she made with her feet and clothing, which made it seem as if a ghost were walking around me. She sat down next to me and put the nest into my hand. As soon as I had it, I saw her again, but she could not see me. This we tried again and again with each other, and found every time that whoever had the nest in his hand was completely invisible. Hereupon she wrapped the little nest in a kerchief, so that the stone or herb or root which was in the nest and had this power might not fall out and perchance be lost. And after she put it down next to her, we saw one another again, as we had before she had climbed up the tree. The kerchief around the nest we did not see, but we could indeed feel it in the place where she had put it.

"I could not but wonder greatly at this, as can easily be imagined, for it was something the likes of which I had never seen or heard of in all my livelong days. However, my wife told me that her parents had often spoken of a fellow who had such a nest and had made himself very rich by its power and effect; namely, he had gone hither and yon to where there was much money and goods, which he had snatched while invisible, and in that way he had gathered together a large treasure. If I therefore were willing, she said, with the aid of this treasure-nest I could help us out of our poverty. I answered: 'This thing is uncertain and dangerous, and it might well happen that somewhere there might be someone who can see more than other people, and by whom we might be found out, and then we'd be hanged by our fine necks. But before I put myself in such danger and in my old age start stealing again, I'd rather burn the nest.' As soon as I had said this and my wife heard it, she snatched up the nest, walked a little ways away from me, and said: 'You silly old son-of-a-bitch! You are worthy neither of me nor of this treasure, and it would really be too bad if you should spend your days other than in poverty and beggary. Do not think that you'll ever see me again in all your life, or that you'll ever enjoy what this nest will bring me!' I, however, begged her, even though I did not see her, not to put herself in danger, but rather to be satisfied with what we received daily from honest folk with our music, so that, after all, we were not obliged to go hungry. She answered: 'Go on! You old shit-arse! Go fuck your mother!' "

CHAPTER 24

What merry cheats and other pranks
the hurdy-gurdy girl perpetrated;
how she became a poltergeist, her husband, however,
a soldier once more, fighting the Turks

"Now when I could no longer either see or hear my wanton wife, I nevertheless shouted after her that she might as well also take along her bundle or pack, which she had left lying next to me, for I well knew that she had no money in it, but rather had our cash sewn into her bodice. Thereupon I took the most direct route to the capital of that country, and although its name sounds almost religious,[1] I nevertheless entered it to seek my sustenance there with the sounds of my worldly shawm and fiddle.

"At that time there were Venetian recruiters there who hired me to attract a crowd for them with my music and with other amusing and amazing juggler's tricks. In addition to food and drink, they gave me a half a sovereign every day, and when they saw that I served their purpose better than any three musicians or any other decoys which they might have wished to employ in order to catch the birds they were after, they persuaded me to take their money and act as if I too had been snared by them. And this brought it to pass that, at my urging, many more were ensnared into military service than would otherwise have gone. We passed our time in nothing but gorging ourselves, swilling liquor, dancing, singing, cavorting, and otherwise making merry, as is customary wherever men are being recruited. But afterwards, in Candia,[2] this hangman's feast profited us about as well as eating grass does a dog, who must suffer because of what he has eaten.

"Once, when I was standing all alone on the square, looking at the beautiful statue of the Virgin there,[3] and not thinking about anything in particular, I felt something heavy roll into my pants pocket, something which made a clinking noise, so that I could hear that they were sovereigns. Now when I put my hand into my pocket and indeed grasped a handful of them, I heard at the same time my wife's voice say to me:

'You old shit-arse! Why are you so surprised at these few dozen sovereigns? I'm giving them to you so that you'll know that I have yet more of them, and so that you'll have cause to grieve that you were unwilling to partake of my good fortune. Now, go on! And use these so that you can forget your misery for a little while.' I said that she should talk further with me, forgive me my mistake, and set forth rules on how I should behave towards her, and thereby be reconciled with her; but she did not let me see or hear anything more of her. I therefore went to my inn and drank brandy with the recruiters and their new recruits till midday, when, during the noon repast, we received news from our innkeeper that a rich gentleman in the city had been robbed of much gold and silver money and jewels, among them a thousand sovereigns and a thousand double ducats of the same minting. I pricked my ears up sharply, took a walk to the privy, as if I had something to do there, but actually to examine my sovereigns, of which there were thirty, and I saw by the look of them that it was my lawfully wedded wife who had made the above-mentioned rich strike. For this reason I took care not to spend any of them, and thereby bring suspicion, danger, and distress upon myself. But what did my wife do, that young crowbait? She stuck her stolen sovereigns not only into my pocket, but into the pockets of a hundred persons of various classes here and there—three into one man's pocket, into another's four, five, six, or more. Now people who were rich, honest, and God-fearing took the money back to its rightful owner, but those who were poor, without conscience, and like me, undoubtedly kept, as I did, what they found in their pockets. And I cannot imagine why she felt compelled to do this, unless the slut simply did not wish to carry such heavy money around with her. Or else it could be that she did it as a joke, to do something which would astound people, for when it got on towards evening, and people were coming from vespers and standing about here and there in the town square, nigh on to two hundred of those same sovereigns were thrown down from above, gathered up by the people, and mostly returned to their owner. The result of this was that the gentleman's innocent servants, who had been suspected of the theft and therefore imprisoned, were set free again. And the gentleman who had been robbed even hoped that his double ducats would turn up again, like his sovereigns, but this did not happen, because lovely gold is much heavier than silver, and *Sol* is not as mobile and capricious as *Luna*.[4]

"The next day a splendid banquet was given at the home of a great gentleman, at which many other great gentlemen and fine ladies were present. They were all sitting in a large and beautiful hall, while the four best musicians in the whole town played for them. Now when dessert was on the table and the dancing was supposed to begin, unexpectedly the sound of a hurdy-gurdy was also heard coming from where the musicians were sitting, to the great consternation of all who were in the hall. The first to run away were the musicians themselves, who heard the rasping sound close by, and yet did not see anyone. They were followed by the rest in great fear, and the press became all the more violent when they were even more affrighted by a sudden peal of laughter coming from the corner where the musicians had been sitting; and it lacked little but that some of them might have been crushed to death at the doorway. Now after everyone had cleared out of the hall in the above-described manner, some, who had stopped outside the door and had the heart to look into the hall from afar, saw how at times a few chairs, at times a few silver goblets, platters, and other tableware were dancing around with each other. And although this tomfoolery came to an end betimes, for a long while nobody had the heart to go back into the hall, despite the fact that clergymen and soldiers had been fetched to drive the ghost away, either by prayer or by main force. But early the next morning, when they went back into the hall and found not a single spoon, much less any of the other silverware, missing—despite the fact that the whole table had been set with it, this strengthened the delusion of the common unthinking rabble to such a degree that those silly wiseacres, who only yesterday, in respect to the strange story concerning the stolen money, had said: 'That's what it takes! It takes sovereigns falling from heaven for money to get back into the hands of the common folk!' now did not shrink from blasphemy, saying: 'The devil himself is obliged to play the music where the sweat of the poor is wantonly wasted!'

"I am obliged to tell one more thing which my second wife, who was even more of a monster than Courage, did, out of sheer revenge, to my way of thinking. Shortly before all this, to please the abbess of a great and rich convent, she had tuned her hurdy-gurdy to play a song for her, and as a matter of fact, a religious one, in hopes of receiving perchance a half or a whole farthing as a reward. But the abbess, instead of listening to the song and then opening her charitable hand, opened her mouth a bit too harshly and sharply, and preached my good little wife a sermon which she found as vexing as she did unpalatable, for it was of such content as is wont to frighten even the most wanton of women, and thereby to force and inspire them to lead a better life. Alas, the good abbess may indeed have meant well, and may have even imagined that she had here a lay sister to reprimand! But no, she had before her another kind of woman, a trump-ace of harlotry! A snake, or even a half-devil, whose tongue I myself many times found sharper than a two-edged sword! ''ods bodikins, Milady! Do you take me then for a whore?' she answered her. 'You must know that I have an honorable husband of my own, and that we cannot all be nuns, or be rich and eat our daily bread in leisure and sloth. If God has blessed you more than me, then give Him thanks for that, and if you don't want to give me any alms for His sake, then at least don't raise cain with me! Who knows whether there would not be more hurdy-gurdy girls than nuns, if so many alms had not been given to the Church, etc.' With these and other words she trundled off. But now the people in the town and in the country could talk of nothing but of the abbess and a poltergeist which plagued her incessantly, day and night, and who was none other than my dear wife! The first thing she did was to take, one night, the abbess' rings from her fingers and the clothes from the bed and to carry them to the bakery, where she put the rings on the baker's fingers and laid Milady's habit at his feet, without anyone hearing or noticing a thing. And this she no doubt accomplished with the master key which she had snatched, for it was lost at about this time. Now one can easily imagine what sort of gossip about the good abbess this caused. People told of many other things which the ghost did to vex the abbess, things against which neither holy water, nor the *agnus dei,*[5] nor anything else was of any avail, but the truth of which the people outside the convent could not determine.

"In the meantime my recruiters had gotten their full complement of men, and whereas I thought that I should be allowed to stay behind, look you, the deceiver was himself deceived, and good old Hopalong was hoist upon his own petard and obliged to hop into the Candian trap he had set for others with his blandishments, except that I was to serve as a corporal of infantry.''

CHAPTER 25

What spoils of war Hopalong got in Candia,[1]
and how he got them;
also, how he came back to Germany

"Thus we, who had sold our lives and yet were determined to fight valiantly to preserve them, made our way over the Zirlberg Pass to Innsbruck, then over the Brenner Pass to Trient, and then on to Treviso, where we were all given new clothes and from there sent all the way to Venice, where we were given arms and, after we had rested a few days, put on board a ship and taken to Candia, at which wretched place we did indeed safely arrive. They did not leave us much time to rest, or for grass to grow under our feet, for the very next day we sallied forth and proved our ability and capacity to help defend our pitiful pile of rocks against the enemy. And in this first engagement I myself was so successful that I spitted three Turks on my half-pike, which seemed to me so trifling and easy to do that to this very day I cannot but think that all three of the poor boobs must have been sick. But taking booty was not possible, because we were obliged to retire straightway to our lines. The next day the fighting was even fiercer, and I killed two more men than the day before, but they were such impoverished ninnies that I did not believe that all five of them together had even a single ducat between them. For it seemed to me that they were such fellows as often were in our army, who were obliged to risk their own lives in order to defend and guard the lives of those who had money; who, on top of that, were obliged to win with their calloused hands and valiant fists the honor of vanquishing the foe; and who were then finally obliged to turn over to those who had money both the honor, the booty, and the rewards of victory. For we never saw a bey or a beylikbey,[2] much less a pasha, among those who were there to wager their blood against Christian blood. But it may be that there were more drivers behind, pushing the troops of that kind, than there were leaders ahead of them.

"This way of waging war made me indignant, and had as a consequence that right there in Candia I was obliged to praise the grateful manner of the Swedes, who esteem their common soldiers (be they foreigners or natives) more highly than their noble but unwarlike countrymen, which is the reason why they have been so very fortunate. But I let them use me in any way and for any purpose, as befits a true soldier. On the fields of battle I fought like an honorable lansquenet,[3] and under them I strove to surpass the moles in their art, and yet got nothing in return for it but a trifling commendation once in a while. And when hardly one man out of ten who had come with me from Germany was still alive, your wretched Hopalong was made sergeant over the even more wretched remnants of his sick comrades, as if his exhausted body and groaning spirit could have thereby been restored to their former strength and courage.

"Now through this I had cause to wear myself out even more. I helped eat the few remaining horses, and for that I worked even harder than these horses had. Now, whereas at that time no enemy musket ball could fell me and no Turkish sabre wound me, look you, a stone from an exploding mine struck my leg so mercilessly that the bone in my calf was crushed like sawdust, and they were obliged to straightway take off my leg above the knee. But this misfortune did not come singly, for while I was lying there as a military patient, having my wound cured, I also got the bloody flux, accompanied by a terrible headache, from which my head was filled with as many delusions as my sickbed was with loathing.

"Nothing was more salubrious for me at that time than that high and low bore witness that I had been the epitome of a good soldier, for with this praise they did not spare other medicines either, even though the Venetians are wont to discard their soldiers like old brooms when they are worn out. But I stayed together with other honest fellows who were still alive and doing their duty, so that they might not have in me an example which might make them lazy and sulky. Now when these men too had grown so sparse in number that finally we could hardly man our posts with more than one or two men who had either retained their health up till now, or at least had regained it, look you, peace came unexpectedly, when we were nigh on to breathing our last.

"After our departure, and after I had suffered much discomfort at sea, we finally arrived in Venice again. Many of us, and among them myself, who had hoped to be crowned there with laurel wreaths and covered with gold, were lodged in a military hospital, where I was obliged to fend for myself as best I could till I was again well and able to hop along on my pegleg.

"Following this, I received my honorable discharge and some little bit of money, for I was not as well paid as if I had been serving the honest Dutch in East India. On the other hand, I was given official permission to beg alms from honest folk, to get enough money to get me home again, and in that fashion I amassed the supply of ducats which I still have, because many a signor and many a pious matron shared rather generously with me on the church steps. I did not need to tell them when I was begging that I had been a soldier in Candia, for they recognized us right off, since almost all of us had lost our hair and look haggard and starved, and as black as the blackest of gypsies. Now because begging was profiting me so well, I kept it up till I got from Venice back to Germany, in the hopes of once more encountering my wife and gladdening her heart that I had learned the begging trade so well, and along with this was bringing along a useful tool for begging, namely, my pegleg. For I thought, this must please her not a little, since she herself was the offspring of the most distinguished clan of arch-beggars.''

CHAPTER 26

*What other pranks the hurdy-gurdy girl played
and how she got her final reward*

"And in order that I might meet up with her, my dear little wife, all the more quickly, I took up with all manner of runagates, vagabonds, and folk of the class with which she had spent the greater part of her life. Among these I diligently inquired after her, but could not find hide nor hair of her. Finally I came to that city in which I had earlier entered into Venetian military service. There I made myself known to the innkeeper and told him how I had since fared in Candia, which innkeeper, being a good old German and a news-hungry man, listened to me very attentively. And when I, in turn, asked what good things had transpired during my absence, he mentioned among other things the ghost which had earlier plagued and vexed the abbess so strangely, but which now, to be sure, had stopped, so that it was supposed that the ghost had been that same mysterious woman whose body had recently been burned not far from there. Now since this was exactly what I wished to know, I not only pricked up my ears, but also bade him tell me the *historia* without further ado.

"Hereupon the innkeeper continued to speak and said: 'At the very time when the abbess was being tormented so by the ghost, and was suspected by all of having illicit intercourse with her *pistor*,[1] other tricks of that kind were played both here in town and out in the country, so that quite a few people thought that the devil himself had been commanded to plague this region. Some folks had their dinners snatched right off the fire; others had their vessels full of wine or beer taken away, some their money, some their clothes, and some even the rings right off their fingers, which things were mostly found again later in other houses, and also in the possession of other people who did not know how they got there, from which any reasonable person might easily conclude that the good abbess had been wronged also. For later on it was nothing unusual any more for someone or other, at night, to have his clothes taken away and different ones put in their place, without anyone knowing how this had happened and come about. Not long afterwards, a baron who lives not far from here celebrated his wedding in a manner worthy, if not of a prince, then at least of a count, at which wedding feast the bride had the splendid dress and jewelry in which she had shone that day, together with her nightgown, taken away from her, and in their place was put a poor woman's dress, full of lice, such as soldiers' women are wont to wear, which event many took to be a sign that the marriage would be an unhappy one, but these prophets only displayed their own ignorance.'

" 'The following month of May, a journeyman baker was strolling one Sunday in a forest about three miles from here, with the intent of looking for birds' nests and taking the young birds. He was a fine, handsome youth, both in face and in physique, and pious and God-fearing besides. Now while he was sneaking upstream along the bank of a little brook, looking about here and there, he espied a woman bathing in the water. He thought it was some girl or other from the village where he was at that time employed; therefore his impudence got the better of him, so that he sat down to wait till she got dressed so that he might recognize her by her clothes, and then might have cause to tease her about having seen her naked. This happened, but not quite exactly the way he had thought, for after this lady had climbed out of the water she did not put on a peasant's smock, but a garment of silver cloth, with golden flowers. After that, she sat down, combed and braided her hair, put precious pearls and other jewels around her neck, and adorned her head with the same kind of jewelry, in such fashion that she looked like a princess. The good baker had observed her up to this time with fear and wonder, and since he was affrighted by her fine appearance, he sought to go away and pretend that he had not seen her at all. But because he was much too close to her, so that she could not but see him, she called out to him, saying: "Listen, young fellow! Are you so un-couth and ill-mannered that you may not approach a maiden?" The baker turned around, doffed his hat, and said: "Milady, I thought it ill fitting that a commoner such as I should approach so grand a lady." "You must not say that," answered the lady, "for one person is as good as another, and moreover, I have been waiting here for you for several hundred years, wherefore God now has finally ordained that we should experi-ence this long awaited hour. So I bid you in God's name to please sit down next to me and hear what I have to tell you." '

" 'At first the baker was afraid, because he feared that it might be a trick of the devil by which he might be seduced into witchcraft; but when he heard her use the name of God, he sat down next to her without trepidation, and she began to speak to him as follows: ''My dearest and most worthy friend, indeed, after God, my only consolation, my only hope, and my only trust! Your dear name is Jacob, and your home town is called Allendorf; and I am Minolanda, the daughter of the sister of Melusina, who bore me by the knight, von Stauffenberg, and placed a curse on me, so that I must remain in this forest from the day I was born till Judgment Day, unless perchance you come to me and choose me as your wife, and thereby deliver me from the curse, but with the express condition and proviso that, above all, you continue, as heretofore, to devote yourself to virtue and to godly ways, eschew the company of all other women, and keep silent about this marriage for a whole year. So now you know what you must do. If you marry me and keep these promises, then I shall not only be delivered from the curse, but shall also bear children like any other woman, and in time depart this world in a state of blessedness; and you shall become the richest and most fortunate man on earth. But if you reject me, then, as you have heard, I must stay here till Judgment Day, and then I shall cry eternal vengeance upon your unmerciful soul, and the fortune which you shall have for the rest of your life shall be such that even the unhappiest of mortals would not wish to share it with you.'' '

'' 'The baker, who had read the story or fable of Melusina and of the knight, von Stauffenberg,[2] and had also heard many other fairy tales about enchanted princesses, believed everything he had been told, and therefore he did not ponder long on it, but willingly said his ''I do'' and consummated the marriage by frequent and repeated fornication with the lady that same day. And she gave him some ducats for the labors he had performed, and took from her neck a little golden cross, set with diamonds and containing holy relics, which she likewise gave to him, so that he might not worry that he had perchance had dealings with a phantom of the devil. And, in the end, it was agreed that she would in the future visit him most nights in his bedchamber, whereupon she vanished before his very eyes.'

'' 'Hardly had four weeks passed when the baker began to feel horror at this whole affair. And when his conscience told him that something must be amiss with this strange and secret marriage, an occasion arose for him to come here and confide everything to his father confessor but outside the confessional. When the latter heard what kind of dress this nixie, or Minolanda, as she called herself, was wearing, and when he remembered withal that just such a dress had been stolen from a noble lady at her nuptials, he pondered further on the matter, and desired also to see the little cross which the baker's doxy had bestowed upon him. When the father confessor saw it, he persuaded the baker to leave it with him just for half an hour, to show it to a jeweler to determine whether the gold be pure, and the stones genuine too. He, however, straightway betook himself with it to the aforementioned lady, who fortunately was here in town, and when she recognized it to be her own, plans were made to lay hold of this Melusina, to which plans the frightened baker gave his consent, promising to help in any way he could.'

" 'Accordingly, on the third night thereafter, twelve stouthearted men armed with halberds were dispatched to take the baker's room by storm at midnight, and to guard closely all the doors and windows, so that if any were opened no one might escape through them. As soon as this had been done, and at the same time two men with torches had entered the room, the baker said to them: "She has already gone!" But hardly were these words out of his mouth when he had a knife with a silver handle sticking in his chest. And before anyone knew it, one of the torchbearers had another knife sticking in his heart, from which he right there fell down dead. One of the armed men calculated from which direction these stabs had come, and therefore jumped back and wielded such a mighty stroke in that direction that he split the Melusina, who was as unlucky as she was invisible, from brisket to bellybutton. In fact, this blow was of such force that not only could one see the oft-mentioned Melusina herself lying there dead, but also her lungs and liver, together with the entrails in her belly, and her heart still beating. Her neck was adorned with jewels, precious rings were on all her fingers, and her head was covered, as it were, with gold and pearls. Otherwise she had on only a shift, a double-taffeta petticoat, and a pair of silk stockings, but the silver dress which had betrayed her lay under her pillow.'

" 'The baker lived till he had made confession and received extreme unction, and afterwards died with great sorrow and remorse, astounded that no money at all had been found[3] on his doxy, whereas she had had more than enough of it. From the looks of her face it was estimated that she was about twenty years old. And her body was burned as that of a witch. The baker, however, was buried in the same grave with the aforementioned torchbearer. As was learned from him shortly before he expired, the slut had spoken a dialect very similar to Austrian.' "

CHAPTER 27

Final conclusion of Hopalong's singular life story

"From this tale I learned what the wonder-working bird's nest had wrought with my wife, how the prickings of her lewd flesh had made her first an adulteress, then a murderess (and, in the end, myself a cuckold), and how it finally brought her herself to a miserable death, yes, even unto the witch's pyre. I asked the innkeeper whether anything else had transpired in conjunction with her. 'Gad!' he answered. 'I almost forgot the best and most noteworthy thing! At her death one of the halberdiers,[1] a lively young fellow, disappeared without a trace, body and soul, hide and hair, clothes and all, so that no one has found out whither he has fled or flown. And this, they say, happened to him when he bent down to pick up a kerchief (which also straightway disappeared) which belonged to that strange woman.' 'Oho!' I thought to myself. 'Now you also know that your little nest has found another owner. May God grant that it benefit him better than it did my wife!'

"I could have dispelled the delusion under which these folk were laboring if I had been of a mind to tell them the truth, but I held my tongue and let them wonder and dispute with one another as long as they liked, and also considered how rudely illusion deceives the ignorant, and what is to be made of the various marvelous tales, which would have been told far differently if their authors had known the true facts.

"Now after I had thus inadvertently learned what had become of my wife, I once more acquired a fiddle and hobbled with it through the Archbishopric of Salzburg, all of Bavaria and Swabia, Franconia and the Wetterau, and through the Lower Palatinate, finally arriving here, everywhere seeking out places where charitable people would give me something. And I am indeed so fortunate at this that I believe that many a one gives me alms who himself does not have one-tenth as much money as I. And because I see that my capital is not diminishing, and I myself can have full freedom to wander wherever I please, to have a full belly and, anytime I need it, a sleek hurdy-gurdy girl as my helpmeet (for birds of a feather flock together), I would not know what might move me to wish for any other or better life, nor how to get such a one. But if you, Simplice, can show me a different and better one, then I should like to hear your advice, and gladly follow it too, depending on what it is."

"I should wish, for your sake," answered Simplicius, "that you would lead your life in the Here and Now in such a manner as not to lose your eternal life in the Hereafter."

"What pious monk's nonsense!" said Hopalong. "It is not possible! You must have been stuck in a cloister sometime, or have in mind soon to crawl into one, that you constantly, contrary to your old ways, talk such silly twiddle-twaddle!"

"If you do not wish to go to Heaven," answered Simplicius, "no one is going to force you to. But I should like it better if you behaved like a good Christian and began to think of your last days, to which you have only a short ways to go."

During this conversation dawn began to break without our noticing it, and this caused all of us to wish to sleep some more, as so frequently happens. This urge we gave way to, and closed our eyes in order to contemplate the inner man for a couple of hours more, and we did not get up till the growling of our stomachs compelled us to eat a few dozen meat pasties and to drink some vermouth. Now as we were engaged in this labor, we received the news that the Rhine had swept away the bridge[2] and was still full of ice, so that no one could go across it in either direction. Therefore Simplicius resolved to stay in the city that day with his family, during which time he would not hear of it that either Hopalong or I leave his company. With me he contracted for me to write down Hopalong's life story as he himself had told it, so that people at the same time should learn that Simplicius' son was not the whoreson of that lewd Courage. And for this he gave me six sovereigns, which I sorely needed at that time. Hopalong he invited to come and spend the winter with him on his farm, assuring me most earnestly, however, that he was not doing this for the sake of Hopalong's few hundred ducats, but rather to see whether he might not induce Hopalong to lead a godly life and follow the path of Christian righteousness. And as I have been told since, this past March did Hopalong in, but not before he, in his old age, had been recast in a different mold by Simplicius and had been moved by him to lead a better, Christian life. And so, this adventurous Hopalong, living on the farm of the equally singular Simplicissimus, and having made the latter his heir, came to his final

END.

Short References Used in the Notes

Garzoni: Garzoni, Tomaso. *Piazza universale, Das ist: Allgemeiner Schawplatz / oder Marckt / und Zusammenkunfft aller Professionen / Künsten / Geschäfften / Händeln und Handwercken / so in der gantzen Welt geübet werden. . . .* Frankfurt am Main: Lucas Jennesius, 1626.

Haberkamm: Haberkamm, Klaus. *"Sensus Astrologicus." Zum Verhältnis von Literatur und Astrologie in Renaissance und Barock.* ("Abhandlungen zur Kunst-, Musik-, und Literaturwissenschaft," Vol. 124.) Bonn: Bouvier, 1972.

Könnecke: Könnecke, Gustav. *Quellen und Forschungen zur Lebensgeschichte Grimmelshausens.* Edited by J. H. Scholte. 2 vols. Weimar: Gesellschaft der Bibliophilen, 1926.

Koschlig (Grimmelshausen und seine Verleger): Koschlig, Manfred. *Grimmelshausen und seine Verleger.* ("Palaestra," Vol. 218.) Leipzig: Akademische Verlagsgesellschaft m. b. H., 1939.

Riederer: Die Simplicianischen Schriften des Hans Jacob Christoffel von Grimmelshausen. Monumentalausgabe in zwei Bänden. Edited by Franz Riederer. Naunhof bei Leipzig: F. W. Hendel, 1939.

Scholte (Springinsfeld): Grimmelshausens Springinsfeld, Abdruck der ältesten Originalausgabe (1670) mit den Lesarten der andern zu Lebzeiten des Verfassers erschienenen Ausgabe. Edited by J. H. Scholte. ("Neudrucke deutscher Literaturwerke des XVI. und XVII. Jahrhunderts," Vols. 249-252.) Halle: Max Niemeyer Verlag, 1928.

Scholte (Zonagri Discurs): Scholte, J. H. *Zonagri Discurs von Waarsagern. Ein Beitrag zu unserer Kenntnis von Grimmelshausens Arbeitsweise. . . .* ("Verhandelingen der koninklijke Akademie van Wetenschappen te Amsterdam, Afdeeling Letterkunde,"* New Series, Vol. 22.) Amsterdam: Johannes Müller, 1921.

Theatrum Europaeum: Theatrum Europaeum. . . . 6 parts. Frankfurt am Main: Wolfgang Hoffmann, 1646-52 and *Theatrum Europaeum. . . .* 20 parts. Frankfurt am Main: various publishers, 1662-1734.

Wassenberg: Wassenberg, Eberhard. *Der ernewerte Teutsche Florus Eberhard Wassenbergs mit Animadversionen, Additionen und Correctionen. . . .* Amsterdam: Ludwig Elzevier, 1647.

Weydt (Nachahmung und Schöpfung im Barock): Weydt, Günther. *Nachahmung und Schöpfung im Barock.* Bern and Munich: Francke Verlag, 1968.

Notes

TITLE PAGE

Hopalong: the name in German, *Springinsfeld,* means "a carefree, heedless person." Könnecke (I, 150 f.) points out that Grimmelshausen may have been inspired to choose the name by a real person, one Jacob Springinsfeld, a drummer from Schwäbisch Gmünd, who on July 31, 1665, registered the birth of a child at Oppenau, a village only a few miles from Gaisbach, where Grimmelshausen at the time lived and served as a steward of the Schauenburg family.

his wondrous MAGIC BOOK: Simplicissimi Magic Book was not printed together with *Heedless Hopalong,* as is indicated here, but rather with another of Grimmelshausen's works, *The First Sluggard.* Koschlig *(Grimmelshausen und seine Verleger,* pp. 223 ff.) assumes, perhaps correctly, that the *Simplicissimi Magic Book* and *The First Sluggard* were published before *Heedless Hopalong* and that Grimmelshausen (or his publisher) included a reference to it here—and perhaps the episodes in which Simplicissimus uses it as well—as additional advertising, as it were.

by Philarcho Grosso von Tromerheim: Philarchus Grossus von Tromerheim, who is also named as the author of *The Runagate Courage* (his name is there spelled "Trommenheim''), is an anagram of Christophorus von Grimmelshausen. Anagrams of another version of the name, Christoffel von Grimmelshausen, were used as names for the alleged authors of other works by Grimmelshausen: Samuel Greifnson vom Hirschfeld *(The Satirical Pilgrim)* and von Hirschfeld *(Chaste Joseph/ Adventurous Musai);* German Schleifheim von Sulsfort *(Simplicissimus);* Michael Rechulin von Sehmsdorff *(The Wondrous Bird's Nest, Part I);* Erich Stainfels von Grufensholm *(Plutus' Council Chamber);* Israel Fromschmit von Hugenfels *(Simplicissimus' Mandrake);* Simon Lengfrisch vom Hartenfels *(The Topsy-Turvy World).* Grimmelshausen even used an anagram of this form of his name as the name of his major hero, Simplicissimus (Melchior Sternfelss von Fuchshaim) and contributed to the mystification of later scholars by noting in the conclusion *(Beschluss)* after Book VI of *Simplicissimus* that the real author of this work was Samuel Greifnson vom Hirschfeld, who for some reason had chosen to hide his identity behind a fictious name made "by transposing the letters'' of his real name. Only three of Grimmelshausen's works appeared under his real name: *Ratio Status,* and the two courtly novels, *Dietwald and Amelinde* and *Proximus and Lympida.*

Paphlagonia: a district in Asia Minor between Pontus and Bithynia. Scholte *(Zonagri Discurs,* p. 76) conjectures that Grimmelshausen found the name in his favorite source book, Garzoni's *Piazza universale* (p. 256). There is, of course, no compelling evidence that Grimmelshausen rather than his publisher chose the name. The actual place of publication was Nuremberg.

Felix Stratiot: a fictitious name. The real publisher was Wolf Eberhard Felssecker. Scholte (*Zonagri Discurs,* p. 75 f.) notes that "Stratiot" in German would be "Krieger" and that "Feliks Krieger" is an anagram of I. I. Felsegkker (W. E. Felssecker's son was named Johann Jonathan).

1670: in this instance the date of publication appears to be accurate. Koschlig (*Grimmelshausen und seine Verleger,* p. 222) believes that *Heedless Hopalong* appeared a few months after *The Runagate Courage,* which he thinks was published in the spring of 1670 at the earliest, the fall of 1670 at the latest.

CHAPTER 1

1. *this past Christmas fair:* the German, *Weihnachtsmess,* refers to the winter fair which was held annually at Strasbourg on St. Martin's Square, and began on St. John the Evangelist's Day, December 27. The action actually takes place on a day in early January 1670. See also Chapter 27, note 2.
2. *contemptuance:* Philarchus is so befuddled that he uses a form which does not exist (in German *Fachtung* instead of *Verachtung*).
3. References to the bitter cold have led some critics to consider *Heedless Hopalong* to be Grimmelshausen's "Winter's Tale." In point of fact, the winter of 1669–70 was one of the coldest in human memory, so cold that the Rhine froze solid in some places.
4. *Capitolio:* a word play on Latin *caput* (head) and *capitol.*
5. *Venus and Vulcan:* Philarchus apparently means that if the lady of the house is against him, the master will surely not employ him. The learned allusion is to the assertion by Cicero (*De natura deorum* III, 59) that one of the four Venuses, the daughter of Jupiter and Dione, was married to Vulcan, whom she betrayed with Mars, the alleged father of her son Anteros.

CHAPTER 2

1. *Conjunctio Saturni, Martis, & Mercurii:* the meeting of Saturn, Mars, and Mercury in the same house of the zodiac. F. Riederer believes that Saturn represents Hopalong; Mars, Simplicissimus; and Mercury, Philarchus (Riederer II, 560). But Klaus Haberkamm is probably correct in equating Saturn with Simplicissimus, Mercury with Philarchus, and Mars with Hopalong (Haberkamm, pp. 86 ff.). It might be noted that Hopalong himself (Chapter 9) implies a comparison between himself and "fleet-footed Mercury." The conjunction of the three planets also agrees with the bitter cold weather: Garzoni notes that "according to Alchindus' rule . . . Saturn, Mars, and Mercury bring bad weather" (Garzoni, p. 95). The three planets were also correlated with three of the traditional seven ages of man (cf. Garzoni, p. 286): Mercury with the second age (*pueritia,* i.e., age 5 to 14), Mars with the fifth (*aeras virilis,* age 41 to 56), and Saturn with the seventh (*aeras decrepita,* age 68 to death). These three do in fact correspond fairly well to the three characters: Mercury to Philarchus, Mars to Simplicissimus, and Saturn to Hopalong.
2. *Chica:* a misspelling of Chilca, a port city in Peru south of Lima. Various seventeenth-century works with which Grimmelshausen was probably acquainted reported that a race of giants lived in Chilca.
3. *Nabuchodonosor:* Daniel 4:33 describes King Nebuchadnezzar during his exile: ". . . and he was driven from men, and did eat grass as oxen, and his body was wet with the dew of heaven, till his hairs were grown like eagles' feathers, and his nails like birds' claws."
4. *theriac:* patent medicine, nostrum, cure-all. *Theriakkrämer* (patent-medicine

salesmen) were frequently the objects of criticism in contemporary satires by such authors as Moscherosch and Aegidius Albertinus. Simplicissimus describes in his own biography his cheats and deceits when circumstances forced him to become for a while such a traveling medicine-man. (*Simplicissimus* IV, 8.)

5. *faeces:* sediment.
6. *Candia:* see Chapter 25, note 1.
7. *dragoons:* a dragoon was a mounted infantryman and thus combined the mobility of the cavalryman with the fire-power of the infantryman. Armed with both pistols and a musket, he could fight either on horseback or on foot. At the time dragoons were classified as infantrymen.
8. *'ods hundred sacks o' rents:* a play on the word "sacraments." In the original the pun is equally far-fetched: "Sack voll Enten" (sack full of ducks) for "Sakramenten." The oath was apparently not an uncommon one at the time, for Moscherosch reproduces it also.

CHAPTER 3

1. *Steward:* Grimmelshausen himself became a steward of the family of his former commanding officer, the von Schauenburgs, after he was mustered out of the army in 1649 and continued to serve in that capacity until 1660. Between 1662 and 1666 he again worked as a steward, this time for a well-to-do Strasbourg doctor. Scholte (*Springinsfeld*, p. x f.) believes that Grimmelshausen is here relating a personal experience which he had when he was a young and inexperienced steward.
2. *laughing Democritus . . . weeping Heraclitus:* according to Seneca (*On Anger* II, 10), Democritus (c. 460-c. 370 B.C.) could never observe the doings of his fellow citizens of Abdera without laughing. (The people of Abdera were famous in classical antiquity for their stupidity and stubbornness.) The legend which made Heraclitus of Ephesus (flourished c. 470 B.C.) the "weeping philosopher" is apocryphal and evidently based on a combination of his theory of flux and a misinterpretation of Theophrastus' term "melancholia," which originally meant "impulsiveness," not "sadness." The contrast of Democritus and Heraclitus as two opposite human types was a favorite topos of seventeenth-century authors.
3. *Seneca:* Roman stoic and tragedian (4 B.C.-65 A.D.) whose works were widely read and whose tragedies were frequently imitated in the seventeenth century. The title of the work referred to is *De tranquillitate animi* and the passage, which is found in Chapter 15, reads: "We ought, therefore, to bring ourselves to believe that all the vices of the mob are not odious but ridiculous, and imitate Democritus rather than Heraclitus. For the latter, whenever he went forth in public places, was wont to weep, the former to laugh; to the one all things human were miseries, to the other, follies."
4. *Zoroastris . . . Nerone:* Zoroaster (Zarathustra), the founder of the official religion of the Persian empire. Pliny reported (VII, 15) that "it is recorded of only one person, Zoroaster, that he laughed on the day he was born." No source in antiquity or later, as far as we can determine, mentions that Nero (ruled 37-68 A.D.) did likewise. Possibly this is Grimmelshausen's own invention. Nero is not mentioned along with Zoroaster in the Heraclitus-Democritus anecdote in Peter Lauremberg's *Acerra philologica,* from which the rest of the sentence is taken almost verbatim.
5. *Jesus Christ, our Saviour . . . wept:* for example, Luke 19:41 and John 11:35.
6. *Blessed are those:* a variant of Matthew 5:4: "Blessed are those who mourn, for they shall be comforted."
7. *Governor of Hanau:* these adventures are described in detail in *Simplicissimus* I, 19 ff.
8. *Duke of Weimar:* Bernhard of Saxe-Weimar (1604-1639) and his troops were in the pay of France from 1635 on, and in 1638 controlled the Rhineland.

9. *Tiberius:* Suetonius (*Lives of the Caesars* III, 62, iii) claimed that Tiberius (42 B.C.–37 A.D.) invented this torture.

10. *German Michel:* name of the stock figure who attacked those who eschewed German words and turns of phrase in favor of foreign ones which were not really intelligible to the average German speaker. Grimmelshausen's own treatise on the abuse of the German language, which appeared in 1673, was entitled *German Michel.*

CHAPTER 4

1. *Stumpf's Swiss Chronicle:* the *Chronik gemeiner Eydgenoschaft* by Johannes Stumpf (1500–1566) was published in 1548 in a folio volume consisting of almost 1,500 pages.

2. *a stone cloak, or even a Spanish one:* "Stone cloak" is a euphemism here for "prison cell." A "Spanish cloak" was a torture instrument, a heavy tub with a hole in the bottom. The prisoner's head was placed through the hole so that the entire weight of the tub bore down on his shoulders.

3. *free city:* Strasbourg. Scholte (*Springinsfeld,* pp. xi–xiii) presents convincing circumstantial evidence that the scene of *Hopalong* is Strasbourg. Conclusive evidence that the "free city" is Strasbourg is discussed in Chapter 27, note 2.

4. *the sixth chapter:* in *Simplicissimus* V, 6 the hero relates:

> There was in Sauerbrunnen a beautiful lady who claimed to be of the nobility, but to my mind she was more *mobilis* than *nobilis;* this mantrap, because she seemed rather sleek of appearance, I courted most diligently, and soon gained not only entrance to her house but also all the pleasures which I might have wished and desired; but I straightway felt disgusted at her wantonness, and therefore pondered how I might rid myself of her in good manner, for it seemed to me that she was more inclined to milk my purse than to get me for a husband; on top of that she pursued me everywhere with alluring, fiery glances and other signs of her burning affection so that I felt ashamed for her sake as well as for my own.

5. *last autumn:* autumn 1669.

6. *Urach:* town in Württemberg which boasted a textile industry of some renown.

CHAPTER 5

1. *Lady of Babylon:* the whore of Babylon. "... and I saw a woman sit upon a scarlet-colored beast full of names of blasphemy, having seven heads and ten horns" (Revelation 17:3).

2. *Milady Libushka:* Courage's given name Libushka (Libussa) is that of the legendary founder of Prague, whom some seventeenth-century writers list together with Penthesilea and other famous women warriors.

3. *the scurviest trick:* Courage's version of the incident: "By shooting blanks from a pistol and using a water-squirt full of blood in *secret* [i.e., while she was in the privy] he made me believe that I had been wounded, so that I was viewed, front and behind, not only by the leech who was supposed to bandage me, but by almost all the people in Sauerbrunnen, who afterwards pointed their fingers at me, sang a song about it, and mocked me in such fashion that I was no longer able to bear the ridicule, but quit Sauerbrunnen and the spa before my cure [she had syphilis] was completed."

4. *Sauerbrunnen:* literally "spa." But the German term has been retained because Grimmelshausen uses it in the sense of a place name. The spa to which he is referring is Griesbach, which is quite near Gaisbach, where Grimmelshausen resided.

5. *Murg River:* Courage's flight takes her northward along the crest of the Black Forest to Baden Baden.

6. *A man who:* the proverb concludes "on his backside."

7. *Horb:* a village on the Neckar River.

8. *Gernsbach:* village in the Murg Valley.

9. *Anacharsis:* a Scythian sage who lived during the sixth century B.C. He was killed by the King of Scythia when he attempted to introduce to h to his c ntrymen customs and innovations with which he had become acquainted during travels in Greece. Grimmelshausen refers to him in his very first work, *The Satirical Pilgrim* (Part II, Section 10: "Concerning War"): ". . . according to *Anacharsis* (of whom *Cicero* says he does not know which was greater, the erudition which he possessed or the envy and malice with which he was persecuted) man's highest good is revenge. . . ." Grimmelshausen may well have borrowed this statement from Guevara's *Vom Hofleben und Feldbau* (p. 255) where it appears in almost the same words.

10. *she will have it printed soon: The Runagate Courage* first appeared in the fall of 1670, i.e., some months after the meeting of Simplicissimus, Hopalong, and Philarchus at the inn in Strasbourg.

CHAPTER 6

1. *Countess:* Courage claims to be the illegitimate child of noble parents (cf. *The Runagate Courage,* Chapter 2).

2. *Apulejo:* Apuleius, the author of *The Golden Ass,* a late Roman novel (c. 155 A.D.).

CHAPTER 7

1. *Perpetual Calendar:* this work by Grimmelshausen appeared in 1670 and contained an illustration depicting all the major Simplician characters.

2. *blew into the book:* the pages of the book were cut in such a way that if one held one's thumb at a certain point on the page only every eighth page would be visible when the pages were riffled. Scholte (*Springinsfeld,* p. xv) reports on his purchase of such a book and quotes the instructions for using it. See also Will Erich Peuckert, "Zu Grimmelshausens 'Springinsfeld,'" *Zeitschrift für deutsche Philologie* 74 (1955), 422–23, where instructions on how to make such a book are quoted from Eberhardt Heinrich Fischer's *Albertus Magnus der Andere und Wahre* (1790).

3. *Sybilla:* Sybilla of Cumae offered to sell the Roman king, Tarquinius Superbus, nine books of prophecy. When he refused them, insisting that the price was too high, she burned three of them and then offered him the remaining six at the same price. Again he refused, and again she burned three books and offered him the remaining ones at the same price. When he refused a third time, she burned two of the remaining books and then offered him the only one left at the price she had demanded for all nine of them. Tarquinius now decided to pay the price. Grimmelshausen doubtless read this anecdote in Garzoni (p. 311).

4. *rabbi:* Grimmelshausen shares the prejudice of his time against other nations and confessions. In the case of Jews he seems to confine his bias to the notion that they are invariably avaricious and dishonest traders.

CHAPTER 8

1. Simplicissimus is here drawing a distinction, doubtless well known to his readers, between *magia naturalis* and *magia ceremonialis*. The latter was essentially necromancy and was considered evil because it involved the aid of the devil. The former, of which Simplicissimus claims to be a practitioner, was defined as a natural effect or event which baffled the untutored observer only because he did not understand how it came about. Garzoni (p. 328 f.) distinguishes between two types of *magia naturalis*, one involving natural (organic) things (roses blooming at Christmas, grapes full ripe in May), and the other involving sleight of hand. Simplicissimus, of course, is adept at both (the wine-improving substance, and the "Magic Book").

2. *man of seventy:* Simplicissimus errs here. Hopalong must be sixty-five at the time.

3. *Simplician "Magic Book":* the *Magic Book* appeared in 1670, together with Grimmelshausen's *The First Sluggard.*

CHAPTER 10

1. *lancers:* part of the heavy cavalry. They wore full armor and were armed with a sword, a brace of pistols, and a lance.

2. *exercitia:* literally, "exercises"; here "tricks" or "performance."

3. *Ambrosio Spinola:* Ambrose Spinola, Marquis de los Balbases (1569–1630), was commander-in-chief of the Spanish army in the Netherlands who attempted to put down a revolt against Spanish rule. Hopalong's chronology is in error here; Spinola acted in the Netherlands only after the United Provinces came into the war in support of the Protestant side.

4. *the enemies of the King:* Moritz Prince of Orange (1567–1625) and his younger brother Frederick Henry Prince of Orange (1584–1647). They were the sons of William the Silent and stadtholders of the Republic of the United Netherlands.

5. *John Rumblygut:* the German, *Schmalhans,* is Grimmelshausen's standard personification for "hunger."

CHAPTER 11

1. *Tilly:* Johann Tzerclaes, Count von Tilly, (1559–1632), took Magdeburg for the Emperor on May 10, 1631. Könnecke (I, 29 f.) discusses another version of the anecdote which, he believes, was well known in Magdeburg during the Thirty Years' War.

2. *Königsmarck:* Hans Christoffer, Count von Königsmarck, (1600–1663) took part of Prague on July 15, 1648. No other version of this anecdote could be found by Könnecke (I, 31); he suspects that Grimmelshausen heard it while visiting Prague.

3. *nor did the Swedes take the city:* the conquest of the old city of Prague was prevented by the conclusion of the Peace of Münster, October 24, 1648.

4. *Holtz:* Georg Friedrich von Holtz (d. 1666) rose through the ranks from a common soldier to a lieutenant field-marshal in the Bavarian army.

5. *Commander Trampius:* the soldier's name in German is "Lumpus," i.e., the word *lump* (rascal, scoundrel, tramp) with the Latin masculine ending *-us*.

6. *musketeer . . . carrying a pike:* the bulk of the infantry consisted at the time of two types of footsoldiers: musketeers and pikemen. Musketeers carried a musket about six feet long and so heavy that it had to be rested on a fork when fired; in addition to his firearm, the musketeer carried a bandoleer with extra powder charges. The pikeman, equipped with a helmet and a breastplate, carried a sword and a pike some eighteen feet long. The pikeman was the least highly regarded of infantrymen (cf. Hopalong's discussion of their plight, Chapter 13).

7.   *during the armistice:* the time shortly after the Peace of Münster is meant. (The terms of the armistice were not completely carried out until June 26, 1650, at Nuremberg.) During 1649 both von Holtz' regiment and the regiment of Elter, in which Grimmelshausen was serving, were stationed at Burglengsfeld, and at this time Grimmelshausen evidently saw Lumpus and learned of his wastrel ways (cf. Könnecke I, 32 f.).

8.   *battle of Herbsthausen:* the Bavarian army defeated Turenne at Herbsthausen, a village on the Tauber River near Mergentheim, May 5, 1645. Courage describes the battle from the point of view of one serving with the other side (*The Runagate Courage,* Chapter 25).

9.   *Bavarian city and fortress:* Ingolstadt, which Gustav Adolph, King of Sweden, had besieged in vain in 1632.

10.   *capital:* Munich.

11.   *Atlas:* a figure of Atlas supporting the heavens was often used as the frontispiece of early collections of maps. (Allegedly it first appeared in Mercator's collection.) The name *Atlas* came to be used as the name for a volume of maps.

12.   *soldier of fortune:* during the Thirty Years' War this term referred to one of common birth who by uncommon valor and considerable good luck had risen to a rank normally reserved for members of the nobility.

CHAPTER 12

1.   *the first one was golden and the other iron:* Hopalong is drawing an analogy to the ages of mankind.

2.   *overran that happy land:* Spinola invaded the Rhenish Palatinate in 1620. Grimmelshausen's source, Wassenberg (p. 29), writes: "But all this was crushed by *Ambrosii Spinolae* unexpected invasion of the Palatinate. He attacked *Frederici patrimonium* and took that happy land as if with a Deluge. And thus, he whom the confederated princes had resisted in vain, in a few short months subjugated more than fifty towns." The ruler of the Palatinate, Frederick, the Elector Palatine, who was the leader of the Protestant Union in Germany, had unwisely chosen to accept the crown offered him by the Bohemian Protestants upon the death of Emperor Matthias (who was also King of Bohemia) in 1619. He also afforded military support to the Bohemian rebels in the form of an army of mercenaries. Spinola's invasion of the Palatinate was the inevitable Habsburg reaction to Frederick's imprudent act. Hopalong's military career thus begins at the onset of the Thirty Years' War.

3.   *Don Gonzales de Cordoba:* became commander-in-chief of the Spanish forces in Germany when Spinola was called back to the Netherlands. Don Gonzales de Cordoba raised the siege of Frankenthal, October 21, 1621.

4.   *Mansfeld:* the army of Count Ernst von Mansfeld (1580–1626). An officer of Archduke Leopold until real or fancied ingratitude drove him into the arms of Habsburg's enemies, Mansfeld crossed into Alsatia after Mannheim had been taken by Tilly on October 23, 1622.

5.   *Tilly's army:* Tilly commanded the army of Maximilian I of Bavaria. When Frederick, the Elector Palatine, accepted the crown of Bohemia, Maximilian allied himself with Emperor Ferdinand in return for a promise of Frederick's prince electorship after the latter's defeat. In 1620 Tilly's forces, together with the Imperial army, invaded Bohemia, soundly defeated the Protestant rebels, and put an end to the reign of Frederick, who was henceforth known in history as the "Winter King." Then, in 1622, Tilly led the Bavarian army into Germany and joined forces with the Spanish Habsburg army in the Palatinate. Hopalong was thus not leaving the Catholic forces, but merely going from one of their armies to the other.

6.   *Wiesloch:* village in Baden where Mansfeld defeated the Bavarian forces under

Tilly, April 26, 1622. Courage lost a husband in this battle (*The Runagate Courage*, Chapter 6).

7. *lad of seventeen:* meaning that Hopalong was born in 1605 and was thus seventeen years older than Simplicissimus, and not seventy years old at the time of his reunion with Simplicissimus, but rather sixty-five.

8. *tirones:* recruits, i.e., the lowest rank of enlisted man.

9. *Wimpfen:* Tilly's army defeated that of the Margrave of Baden at Wimpfen, May 6, 1622. Courage also took part in this "almost merry battle" (*The Runagate Courage*, Chapter 7).

10. *at the Main River:* Tilly defeated Prince Christian of Brunswick, administrator of the secularized bishopric of Halberstadt, at Höchst, a city on the Main, June 20, 1622. Courage also describes her exploits in this battle (*The Runagate Courage*, Chapter 8). Moreover, Simplicissimus was born shortly after this battle (*Simplicissimus* I, 22; V, 8).

11. *Stadtlohe:* Stadtlohn, a town in Westphalia quite near the Dutch border, where Tilly decisively defeated Prince Christian of Brunswick, August 6, 1623.

12. *Danish war in Holstein:* this phase of the Thirty Years' War lasted from 1625 to 1629.

13. *Lutter:* Lutter am Bärenberg in the Duchy of Brunswick, where Tilly defeated Christian IV, King of Denmark, August 27, 1626.

14. *Steinbruck... other towns:* Steinbruck, north of Hildesheim; Verden on the Aller; Langwedel, not far from Verden; Rotenburg on the Wumme; and Ottersberg, situated between Bremen and Rotenburg. One of the other towns, mentioned by name by Courage, was Hoya on the Weser (*The Runagate Courage*, Chapter 11).

15. *salva guardi:* garrison duty.

16. *Farter General:* Courage reports that she was called "the General Fartress, because I do it better than anyone else" (*The Runagate Courage*, Chapter 17). To be sure, her flatulence is the result of a trick played on her by rival courtesans. Hopalong's remarks here repeat nearly verbatim an anecdote which Grimmelshausen included in his *Perpetual Calendar* under December 29: "I knew a drummer who could,... while lying on a bench, blow taps for a whole hour."

17. *Seyfried with the Horny Skin:* the hero of a popular chapbook which appeared around 1630 and which presented in prose the adventures of Siegfried, the hero of the *Nibelungenlied*. By bathing in the blood of a dragon which he had slain, Siegfried acquired a skin which could not be penetrated by sword or spear. His vulnerable spot was a small area on his back where a linden leaf had kept the dragon blood from "arming" the skin.

18. *Cymbrian Cheronesum:* Schleswig-Holstein peninsula.

CHAPTER 13

1. *Swiss miles:* a Swiss mile was 4,800 meters.

2. *Courage... saddled me with that name:* the last point in the contract which Courage required of Hopalong before she would agree to become his common-law wife was: "And so that he might remember his duty toward me at all times, he was to suffer, as a seventh point, that I call him by a special name, which name was to be formed from the first words of the command by which I should the first time order him to do something." Her first command, which Courage gave him so as to be rid of him while she enjoyed a handsome young cornet for whom she lusted, was: "Hop along and catch our piebald! The cornet here would like to ride him and bargain for him for cash."

3. *her fine biography:* Courage gives her version of her life with Hopalong in some detail (*The Runagate Courage*, Chapters 14–22).

4. *when she had grown tired of me:* Courage tells quite a different story. She main-

tains that Hopalong beat her while pretending to have a nightmare and later attempted to throw her into a campfire during another nightmare. She obviously suspected that he was acting in this manner in order to gain over her that control which he had renounced forever in the common-law marriage contract.

5. *bottle imp:* Courage describes it as "some sort of something in a little sealed glass flask that did not rightly look like a spider or like a scorpion either" which she at first thought might present "the likeness of I know now what kind of perpetual motion, because it stirred and crawled about in the flask without rest." The old soldier who sold it to her warned her that "it has a certain price at which it must be bought and sold, for which reason Madam must be careful when she in turn sells it, for she must needs sell it for less than she paid for it." After she has bought it, the seller tells her that it is "a servant-spirit which brings great good fortune to that person who buys it and keeps it with him. . . . it brings good fortune, victory, and conquest over the enemy, and makes it necessary that almost everyone love its owner," but from her old Bohemian nurse Courage learns that "the last one who buys it must fall prey to it" and will suffer eternal damnation. When Courage and Hopalong parted ways, there was included in their separation agreement the stipulation that Hopalong would buy the "*Spiritus famil.*" for one crown, and Courage exulted at the difficulty Hopalong had getting rid of it.

6. *von Altringen:* Johann Count von Aldringer (1588–1634), together with Rambold XIII, Count di Collalto (1579–1630) and Matthias Count von Gallas (1589–1647), had marched into Italy in 1629 with an Imperial army, to which Hopalong and Courage had been attached as sutlers. Aldringer's army returned to Württemberg in 1631 after the Peace of Nevers (*The Runagate Courage,* Chapter 14 ff.).

7. *captured by the Swedes:* in July 1630 Gustavus Adolphus, King of Sweden, who had entered the war on the Protestant side, invaded Germany with his well-disciplined army. He defeated Tilly at Breitenfeld near Leipzig and then proceeded to take the Rhineland.

8. *the Imperials got their hands on me again:* Hopalong means the Imperial army proper, not that of Habsburg's ally, Bavaria.

9. *Würzburg . . . other towns:* Gustav Adolph took Würzburg on October 14, 1631, Aschaffenburg on November 22, and Mainz on December 20; during the campaign Bernhard of Saxe-Weimar took Mannheim. Wassenberg (pp. 266–68) mentions all these towns, including Bacharach, in his description of the campaign.

10. *von Pappenheim:* Gottfried Heinrich, Count zu Pappenheim (1594–1632), one of the most famous and valiant generals of the Imperial army, occupied Westphalia in 1631.

11. *Prince Elector of Cologne:* Ferdinand, Prince Elector and Archbishop of Cologne (1577–1650), was the son of William V, Duke of Bavaria, and the brother of the next duke, Maximilian I.

12. *Swabian lad:* Hopalong evidently has in mind the legendary Swiss hero Arnold Winkelried.

13. *General Bannier:* the Swedish general Johan Banér (1596–1641) withdrew from Magdeburg in January 1632, leaving it for von Pappenheim to occupy.

CHAPTER 14

1. *corpo:* Latin for "army." The use of the wrong case here, according to Weydt (*Nachahmung und Schöpfung im Barock,* p. 24), does not prove that Grimmelshausen knew little or no Latin, but rather is Grimmelshausen's attempt to give the flavor of Latin words which were used—and misused—by soldiers during the Thirty Years' War. The term *corpo* does in fact occur repeatedly in Grimmelshausen's two primary historical sources, the *Theatrum Europaeum* and Wassenberg.

2. *Lemgo . . . other cities:* Pappenheim's Westphalian campaign took place in spring of 1632.

3. *Duke George of Lüneburg:* Pappenheim's army defeated the armies of both Baner and Duke George of Brunswick-Lüneburg (1582–1641) in February 1632.

4. *Stade:* Pappenheim's forces relieved Stade, a town on the lower Elbe which had been under siege by the Swedish General Tott, in March 1632.

5. *my money and my good fortune:* this is the high point of Hopalong's military career, the closest he comes to the goal of many seventeenth-century military men who as commoners could not be appointed to an officer's rank unless their valor and good fortune in battle attracted the attention of the general staff or enabled them to raise and equip a military unit of their own.

6. *Maestricht:* the Dutch, led by Duke Henry of Orange, had seized the fortress of Maestricht in 1632. Pappenheim's attempts to retake it in August 1632 were in vain.

7. *the Hessian and Baudis:* the "Hessian" was Landgrave William V of Hesse-Cassel (d. 1637). "Baudis" refers to Wolf Heinrich von Baudissin of the house of Luppau (1579–1646), a field marshal in the Swedish army and a direct ancestor of the poet of the same name who assisted in the Schlegel-Tieck translation of the works of Shakespeare.

8. *seek protection:* the incident occurred in September 1632.

9. *Hildesheim:* Pappenheim conquered Hildesheim on September 28, 1632, and joined forces with Wallenstein's army on November 6.

10. *myrrh and rue:* myrrh was the symbol of death; rue, that of poverty.

11. *pyrc:* finished, "kaput."

12. *Memmingen and Kempten:* towns in the Allgäu in Bavaria taken by Aldringer's troops in January 1633.

13. *Forbus:* Sir William Forbes, a Scot by birth who served as a general in the Swedish army, was defeated by Aldringer and taken prisoner in April 1633.

14. *a niemezy or niemey:* a German. Hopalong (or Grimmelshausen) apparently no longer recalls which form is correct.

CHAPTER 15

1. *Wallenstein . . . Eger:* the assassination took place on February 25, 1634.

2. *Ferdinand III:* Ferdinand III (1608–1657), who reigned as Emperor from 1637 until his death, had become King of Hungary in 1625 and King of Bohemia in 1627.

3. *Regensburg:* Ferdinand's army besieged Regensburg from May 15 to July 17, 1634.

4. *Johann de Werdt:* Jean Count de Werth (Werth or Werd; also called Joan von Werd) (1600–1652) is mentioned by Grimmelshausen in *The Satirical Pilgrim* (Part II, Section 10: "On War"), and repeatedly in the later Simplician works. Wassenberg (p. 317), ever partisan to the Imperial side, characterizes de Werdt:

> This renowned commander had been a common soldier under the King of Spain in the Netherlands, and afterwards under the Emperor was promoted through the ranks to captain-of-horse, and threw a scare into the enemy with his lone company of horse as if it had been a whole regiment. Therefore he was worthy of a regimental command, and when he was given it, he was so frightening, with all sorts of weapons and wondrous alacrity, that when people merely mentioned his name and heard of his arrival, thousands of them took fright and trembled with fear. . . . He continued with this way of his of making war almost as if a second Phoenix had come forth from the ashes of the brave *Godefridi Henrici* Count von Pappenheim.

5. *Gustav Horn:* Gustaf Karlsson (af Bjorneborg), Count Horn, (1592–1657), who held the rank of field marshal at the time, had joined Bernhard of Saxe-Weimar in an attempt to raise the siege.
6. *Landshut:* the battle took place on July 22, 1634. The remark about "the bridge at Landshut" was doubtless inspired by Wassenberg's reference (p. 332) to it and to Aldringer's death in the fray.
7. *Ries:* the so-called "Nördlinger Ries," a fertile region on the Swabian-Bavarian border. The Cardinal Infant had brought his army from the Trientine Mountains into Germany and joined forces with Ferdinand III there.
8. *Nördlingen:* the siege began on August 18, 1634.
9. *a very bloody battle:* the Battle of Nördlingen, in which the Imperial forces defeated the armies of Bernhard of Saxe-Weimar and Marshal Horn, took place on September 6–7, 1634.
10. *the Lothringian:* Duke Charles III of Lorraine (1604–1675). The source is Wassenberg (p. 337): "But they [the Protestant armies] were chased back again with great losses by His Highness *Carolo* Duke of Lorraine and *Johanne de Werd,* by the Croats and the Hungarians."
11. *a lowly sluggard can take the life of the bravest hero:* Grimmelshausen makes the same point in *The Satirical Pilgrim* (Part II, Section 2: "On Guns"), and in *Simplicissimus* III, 12. The thought, of course, is by no means original with him. Moscherosch, to name only one, makes the same point in "Soldiers' Life."

CHAPTER 16

1. *harmonia:* melody played by two or more instruments.
2. *Speyer . . . other towns:* these actions took place in 1635. Wassenberg (pp. 411 ff.) also describes the horrors of the famine and pestilence suffered by the Rhineland at this time.
3. *Count Philipp von Mansfeld:* Imperial general whose army took Frankenthal on December 25, 1636, after a prolonged siege.
4. *Spanish reals, English Jacobuses, rose ryals:* the German is unclear here, but the large English gold coin which Hopalong calls *Umgicker* may well be "rose ryals." The rose ryal was a large coin worth thirty shillings and containing 213⅓ grains of fine (24 carat) gold; it had, on the obverse, James I seated on the throne, full face, and he appears to be squinting at something (i.e., *ein Umgucker*). The Jacobus (also called the "sovereign" and the "unite") was a large gold coin, just under 155 grains, of crown (22 carat) gold. If Hopalong was considering rose ryals equal in value to sovereigns, he was cheating himself at the outset. When one considers that the sovereign was worth thirty shillings while the silver crown was equivalent to only five shillings, it is clear that Hopalong cheated himself yet again in presuming his gold coins to be worth two or three silver ones. In fact, his gold coins were worth at least four to six silver ones. (Cf. C. V. H. Sutherland, *English Coinage 600–1900,* London: Batsford, 1973, p. 159; Plates 76 and 77.)
5. *Count von Götz:* Johann Count von Götz (1599–1645) took over command of the Imperial army formerly led by Count von Gronsfeld, drove Landgrave William of Hesse out of Westphalia, and occupied that land in 1636–37. During this period Grimmelshausen was serving as a musketeer in Götz's army.
6. *Dortmund . . . others:* here Grimmelshausen is able to give a more complete list of towns taken by Götz than is found in the *Theatrum Europaeum* and in Wassenberg's book.
7. *no need to tell about:* the adventures which Simplicissimus and Hopalong shared are described in *Simplicissimus* II and III.
8. *Colonel S. Andreas:* Daniel von St. Andrée, a Hessian colonel who campaigned in Westphalia in 1637, was not actually the commandant of Lippstadt at the time of

the attack, January 25, 1638. He had been replaced as commanding officer by Colonel Renssen. See also *Simplicissimus* III, 15.

9. *My savings . . . Coesfeld:* Hopalong is required to change sides, now to serve with the Protestant forces. Imperial successes on the field of battle had moved Richelieu to bring France back into the war, which from then on became less a religious war and more a political one, a dynastic struggle for survival between the Bourbons of France and the Habsburgs of Austria and Spain.

10. *Cologne:* the invasion occurred in November 1641.

11. *Lampoy:* Wilhelm Count von Lamboy (d. 1659), a favorite of Wallenstein best known for his siege of Hanau in 1636, was defeated by the French under the command of Lieutenant General Jean Baptiste de Budes, Comte de Guebriant, on January 17, 1642. The battle took place at Kempen, a town near Crefeld.

12. *Lechenich:* the main fortified town of the Archbishopric of Cologne in Westphalia. It was besieged by the Weimar forces in 1642.

13. *Zons:* fortified town in Westphalia on the left bank of the Rhine.

14. *Guebriant . . . Franconia:* According to Wassenberg (p. 508), Guebriant (1602–1643) led his army from the Rhine through the Thuringian Forest into Franconia in early 1643.

15. *Schorndorf:* the engagement in this town in the Rems Valley took place on January 21, 1643.

16. *I was taken prisoner:* Hopalong changes sides, now for the last time, for he finishes the war in the Catholic forces.

17. *Bugger:* the real name of the officer in question was Wilhelm Balthasar Kurnreuther, a lieutenant colonel in the Bavarian army whom the soldiers nicknamed "Kirbereuther" (*Kerbenreiter*) because of his alleged homosexual proclivities. The inspiration for this passage may have been Wassenberg's account (p. 515): ". . . Lieutenant-Colonel Kürmreutter brought over one hundred enemy prisoners, together with a large number of horses, into the Bavarian camp, on which occasion some of the Bavarian war-officers got booty in the amount from two or three up to ten thousand sovereigns and also other fine things. . . ."

18. *Reinhold von Rosen:* all the details of the action are taken from *Theatrum Europaeum* V, 185 f.: "Meanwhile the otherwise bold and proven military commander Reinhold von Rosen, following orders, on 18th of this month [October 1643] appeared before the city of Ballingen with four regiments under his sole command . . . totaling 1,200 horse, with the intention of occupying the town. But he had to withdraw again."

19. *I saw a large wolf:* the story of Hopalong's battle with the wolves was probably inspired by an incident which occurred in Gelnhausen, Grimmelshausen's home town, and which was reported in *Theatrum Europaeum* III, 770 f.

CHAPTER 17

1. *Colonel Sporck's regiment:* Johann Count von Sporck (c. 1600–1679).

2. *Rottweil:* a town located between the Black Forest and the Swabian Alb, on the left bank of the upper course of the Neckar River. It was taken on November 18, 1643, by Guebriant, who died a week later from wounds received while storming the town.

3. *Tuttlingen Fair:* battle fought at Tuttlingen, a town on the Danube in Württemberg, on December 3, 1643, in which the French army led by General Rantzau was destroyed by the Imperialists.

4. *General von Mercy:* Franz Freiherr von Mercy (c. 1590–1645) retook Rottweil on December 13, 1643. Hopalong's actions as the baggage train was leaving were probably inspired by Wassenberg's remark (p. 551) that "the departing baggage suffered some damage, despite the fact that the field marshal had some soldiers shot for it."

5. *retook . . . per accord:* the city was reoccupied after negotiations in which conditions were agreed upon for the withdrawal of the defenders from the city (as opposed to the "unconditional surrender" of a city or the taking of a city "by storm").

CHAPTER 18

1. *Überlingen:* the town surrendered on May 10, 1644, after a two-month siege, and was occupied by von Holtz' regiment.
2. *Freiburg:* taken by von Mercy on July 28, 1644.
3. *Duc d'Enghien:* Louis II of Bourbon (1621–1686) bore this title until the death of his father in 1646, at which time he assumed the family title, Prince de Conde.
4. *Turenne:* Henri de la Tour d'Auvergne, Vicomte de Turenne (1611–1675).
5. *by storming the bulwarks:* the battle took place on August 3 and 5, 1644. Grimmelshausen's sources emphasized the bitterness of the conflict and probably inspired the snow metaphor: ". . . and so many of them were killed that it was downright unbelievable, since they [the French] fell just like snowflakes when they tried to climb up the hill" (Wassenberg, p. 588). And ". . . such a number of French soldiers were killed that it was downright unbelievable, for they fell almost like snowflakes when they tried to climb the hill" (*Theatrum Europaeum* V, 449).
6. *cuirassiers:* together with the lancers they made up the heavy cavalry. They were armed with a brace of pistols and a sword, and wore full armor.
7. *Mannheim:* the city fell in early October 1644.
8. *Höchst:* taken on November 8, 1644.
9. *Bensheim:* town on the Bergstrasse, taken on November 21, 1644. Wassenberg (p. 600) and *Theatrum Europaeum* (V, 604 f.) both describe the death of the Bavarian Colonel of the Dragoons, Johann Wolff, who was presumably Hopalong's commanding officer at the time.
10. *we wreaked havoc:* the Bavarian forces, beginning with the campaign of Götz in Westphalia, had earned the dubious distinction of being more vicious and more prone to pillage, rape, and arson than other armies. In Bensheim they nearly outdid themselves: ". . . the little town of Bensheim was bombarded and a breach in the walls effected, but the invaders climbed over the walls on ladders at other places and got in, and they killed everyone who was armed and completely plundered the town, on which occasion a good many on both sides lost their lives and nearly twenty houses were burned down" (*Theatrum Europaeum* V, 605).
11. *Prince Elector of Bavaria:* Maximilian I.
12. *tirones:* recruits.
13. *Jankau:* the battle took place on February 23, 1645; with it the military career of Simplicissimus, who was fighting on the Imperial side, came to an end (*Simplicissimus* III, 15).
14. *Nagold:* taken by the French on April 4, 1645. The commanding officer to whom Hopalong refers was Colonel Nussbaum, who died of six bullet wounds. Neither Wassenberg nor *Theatrum Europaeum* mentions that Nussbaum's lack of caution was responsible for the French victory.
15. *Herbsthausen:* the battle took place on May 5, 1645. For Courage's reaction to it, see *The Runagate Courage,* Chapter 26. *Theatrum Europaeum* (V, 769) lists by name a field marshal and three generals who were captured, and notes that 204 other officers and about 2,500 troopers and footsoldiers were also taken prisoner.

CHAPTER 19

1. *Amöneburg:* a fortress on a cliff above the Ohm River in Hesse. Amöneburg had been blockaded for seven months before it was succoured by Bavarian forces on about May 25, 1645.

2. *Kirchhain:* a village in the Amöneburg basin at the confluence of the Klein, the Wohra and the Ohm. It was defended by a force of 900 men.
3. *Count von Geleen:* Gottfried Huyn Count von Geleen und Amsterstad (d. 1657).
4. *my colonel:* Hopalong's commanding officer at this juncture was Colonel Creutz. Cf. Wassenberg, p. 643: "... the city of Heilbronn, in which there were 2,000 men under Colonels Fugger, Creutz, and Caspar." Caspar's real name was Caspar Schoch.
5. *Wimpfen:* Turenne's forces took the city on July 8, 1645.
6. *Rothenburg:* according to Grimmelshausen's favorite source, Wassenberg (pp. 635 ff.), Rothenburg on the Tauber was defended at this time by a 200-man unit of dragoons under the command of one of Colonel Creutz's lieutenants.
7. *Allersheim:* a village to the east of Nördlingen. The battle was fought on August 3, 1645.
8. *Nördlingen ... Dinkelsbühl:* Nördlingen capitulated on August 8, 1645. Dinkelsbühl surrendered on August 24. Wassenberg (p. 642) gives the size of the garrison as 400 dragoons and 200 musketeers, and notes that it was under the command of a major of Colonel Creutz's regiment. *Theatrum Europaeum* (V, 859 f.) identifies this officer as Wilhelm Gottfried von Heses.
9. *Archduke Leopold Wilhelm:* the son of Emperor Ferdinand II and brother of Emperor Ferdinand III.
10. *Philippsburg ... Wimpfen:* Wimpfen was retaken on October 26, 1645. Wassenberg (p. 648) is apparently the source for the information about the artillery pieces which were captured.
11. *the following summer:* the summer of 1646.
12. *Wetterau:* the southernmost part of the west Hessian lowlands, between the Taunus Mountains and the Vogelsberg. Almost devoid of forests, it was, even in Grimmelshausen's time, a fruitful plain.
13. *a merry little martial exercitium:* presumably the raid which 1,000 Imperials carried out on June 26, 1646, on sixteen Hessians who were garrisoned in the village of Alsbach (cf. *Theatrum Europaeum* V, 1138).
14. *our commanding officer:* Colonel Georg Creutz.
15. *Jung-Kolb:* the nickname of Hans-Jakob von Reindorff, commander of a regiment of harquebusiers.
16. *Schwabenhausen:* possibly a misspelling of Schrobenhausen, a town on the Paar between Augsburg and Ingolstadt. Wassenberg (p. 708) is Grimmelshausen's source in this instance, for he too writes "Schwabenhausen." *Theatrum Europaeum* (V, 1198 f.) identifies the village as *Pfaffenhofen*, which was also located between Augsburg and Ingolstadt, but on the Ilm River.
17. *Colonel Rouyer:* Frantz (Franciscus) Royer was at this time commanding officer of a regiment of dragoons. Wassenberg (p. 708) asserts that on September 26, 1646, Royer managed to slip through the enemy surrounding Augsburg and get safely into the city with 350 (not 450, as Hopalong says) of his men.
18. *a sort of half-way peace:* a neutrality agreement was signed on March 14, 1647. But Prince Elector Maximilian I of Bavaria declared it void on September 14, whereupon hostilities were resumed.
19. *Deggendorf:* a town on the Danube in lower Bavaria.
20. *several of our generals:* among the commanding officers in question were Jean de Werdt, Colonel von Sporck, and Hopalong's own colonel, Georg Creutz.
21. *his great Prince Elector:* Maximilian I of Bavaria.
22. *the infamous title:* in March 1648 the Prince Elector ordered that Creutz's name be posted on all gallows-trees with the information that Creutz was "a common highwayman and a fellow forgetful of all duties and personal honor" (cited by Könnecke I, 74 f.). In Grimmelshausen's time, St. Nikola was a village (actually a settlement of the Augustine order with attendant buildings) on the outskirts of Passau. Könnecke is convinced that Grimmelshausen, who was stationed in 1648

in Vilshofen, a village on the Danube not far from Passau, is here putting his own personal experiences into Hopalong's mouth.

CHAPTER 20

1. *Melander:* Peter Eppelmann (1585-1648), Count Holzapfel (Holsappel), the Greek form of which, Melander, he used as a name. He was first an officer in the Hessian forces, but in 1641 he left Hessian service and became a commander in the Imperial army. Grimmelshausen's opinion of Melander's abilities may have been influenced by gossip he heard from fellow soldiers and officers. Holzapfel-Melander was killed at the battle of Zusmarshausen on May 17, 1648 and was succeeded by von Gronsfeld.

2. *von Gronsfeld:* Jobst Count von Gronsfeld (d. 1662) became field marshal of the Bavarian forces in 1646 and assumed Melander's command upon the latter's death in 1648.

3. *Wasserburg:* fortified town on the Inn River in Upper Bavaria. Grimmelshausen was himself stationed there.

4. *Mühldorf:* town on the Inn in Upper Bavaria.

5. *one of the von Hunoltsteins:* possibly Hans Wilhelm von Hunoltstein (d. after 1648), who replaced von Gronsfeld as commander of the Bavarian army after the latter was dismissed and imprisoned.

6. *Pfarrkirchen:* town in Lower Bavaria in the Rottal.

7. *Hilpoldstein:* towns in Middle Franconia.

8. *a corporal who wanted to be colonel:* Andreas Walther, called by his peers the "Swedish corporal." The regimental clerk was Hans Georg Halsspacher. Both were enlisted men in the regiment of dragoons commanded by Colonel Bärthel which occupied Hilpoltstein and Heideck at the time of the revolt, April 1649. Walther and his followers fired on some officers and so frightened Bärthel that he promised to discharge them from service immediately with two-and-one-half months' pay. Bärthel went so far as to pledge the lives of his own wife and children as guarantee. When news of the revolt reached headquarters, Field Marshal Enkenvoirt dispatched Colonel von Elter and his regiment (in which Grimmelshausen was then serving as a clerk) to put down the revolt. Hopalong's account of the quelling of the revolt and the punishment of the mutineers agrees with that in *Theatrum Europaeum* and provides some additional details.

CHAPTER 21

1. *the country where all sorts of confessions are permitted:* the Palatinate.

2. *the first capture of the fortress at Frankenthal:* 1621.

3. *fine innkeeper in a very fine inn:* Grimmelshausen on two occasions was forced to earn his livelihood as an innkeeper, first between 1660-62, after he had left the employ of the von Schauenburg family, and again from 1666-67, after he gave up his post as steward for Dr. Kueffer. He was thus familiar with many of the practices, both honest and not so honest, of the trade.

4. *act the Jew:* Grimmelshausen shares the prejudice of his time. Cf. Chapter 7, note 4.

5. *peace tax:* at the Peace of Westphalia, Sweden had demanded and been granted five million sovereigns in reparations, which monies were raised by imposing an oppressive tax on the Germans.

6. *Count von Serini:* Miklos (Nicholas) Count Zrinyi (1620-1664), a Hungarian general and poet who fought against the Turks from 1652 until his death. Hopalong's life as a civilian lasted from 1649 to 1664, fifteen years.

CHAPTER 22

1. *French volunteers:* they joined the war in early 1664.
2. *full-scale battle:* probably the capture of the bridge at Gotthard on February 1, 1664.
3. *oleum populeum:* oil of poplar (tree).
4. *unexpected conclusion of peace:* the Peace of Vasvar (Eisenberg) concluded on August 10, 1664.
5. *Bastion of Christendom:* Hungary.
6. *crippled children:* possibly personal experience inspired the description of the beggar family's infirm and crippled children. In *The Satirical Pilgrim* (Part II, Section 9: "On Begging and Beggars"), Grimmelshausen tells an anecdote about "a blind beggar whom old folks in our neighborhood can recall" who

   had by his wife several children, all of whom he lamed or made cripples while they were still nursing at their mother's breast, until finally the mother gave birth to a beautiful baby boy, for whom she succeeded in getting a respected lady to be godmother. Now when the blind man, as was his wont, was about to break this child's legs, the wife's maternal heart rebelled, and she called on its godmother for help, who sharply reprimanded the blind man and threatened to tell the authorities, to which he merely replied that he had thought to make his son a gentleman, but since she was unwilling, the child could remain a poor devil his whole life long.

7. *conceited old ass that I was:* Hopalong was fifty-nine or sixty years old at the time.
8. *morning gift:* the *Morgengabe* was a gift bestowed by the bridegroom on his bride immediately following the nuptials and remained the sole property of the wife. It was intended to afford her support in the event that her husband predeceased her. In time it came to be looked upon as the husband's payment to his wife for having taken her maidenhead, and it is this interpretation which the hurdy-gurdy girl has in mind.

CHAPTER 23

1. *annual country and religious fairs:* fairs at this time were of two kinds. The *Jahrmarkt* (literally, "annual market"), which was similar to present-day county fairs, was held once each year at a fixed time established by tradition. The *Kirchweihe* (literally, "church consecration") was a popular festival held annually on the anniversary of the consecration of the local church or cathedral.
2. *strap game:* the object of this game (the *Riemenspiel*) was to stick a knife through a rolled-up strap or belt. The strap, however, was rolled up in such a way that the player almost invariably failed, and thus won no prize.
3. Popular superstition was the source for the magic bird's nest. Bächtold-Stäubli, *Handwörterbuch des deutschen Aberglaubens* (VIII, 1459), discusses the popular conviction that there was a stone which could render its bearer invisible and that the stone was to be found in a sisken's nest. The only way the nest itself could be found was to see its shadow reflected.

CHAPTER 24

1. *name sounds almost religious:* the city is Munich, the German form of which, *München,* sounds like the German word for monks, *Mönche. München* does in fact derive from the phrase *zu den munechen,* i.e., "at the place where the monks are."

2. *Candia:* see Chapter 25, note 1.
3. *the beautiful statue of the Virgin there:* the statue erected in 1638 on the Schrannenplatz in Munich (later called Marienplatz). The statue, made of bronze, was mounted atop a column of red marble some twenty feet high.
4. *Sol . . . Luna:* Sol (the sun) is the symbol for gold; Luna (the moon), that for silver.
5. *agnus dei:* Lamb of God, here referring to a medallion with the Lamb of God on it. Such medals were thought to be efficacious in driving out devils and were excellent "life insurance" during witch-hunts, since it was thought that a witch or warlock could not bear to carry one on his or her person.

CHAPTER 25

1. *Candia:* the capital city of Crete. It was taken by the Turks in 1669 after years of siege and the loss of 150,000 men. A company of soldiers recruited at the behest of Franz Egon von Fürstenberg, Bishop of Strasbourg, arrived in Candia in August 1669 and participated in the last battle for that fortified city. In April 1670 Major de Crequeville, the company's commanding officer, returned to Germany with twenty of the 100 men who had gone with him to fight in Crete. It is possible that he and/or some of the other survivors may have stopped in Renchen where Grimmelshausen, who was at that time in the employ of the Bishop of Strasbourg, could have seen and talked with them. Hopalong's marriage to the hurdy-gurdy girl, it might be noted, apparently lasted only about five years.
2. *a bey or a beylikbey:* in the Ottoman Empire a bey was the governor of a district, a beylikbey (beylerbey or beglebeg) the governor of a province, and a pasha a military commander.
3. *lansquenet:* mercenary foot soldier (from the German *Landsknecht*).

CHAPTER 26

1. *pistor:* Latin for "baker."
2. *the fable of Melusina and of the Knight, von Stauffenberg:* Grimmelshausen has here conflated two legends well known in his time. The story of Melusina, the water nymph who promised the Count of Poitiers fame and wealth on the condition that he not attempt to learn her identity or what she did on a specific day of the week (curiosity got the better of him, with unfortunate results for him), was translated into German from the original French in 1456 by Thüring von Ringoltingen and soon became a popular chapbook. The legend of Knight Peter von Stauffenberg was treated around 1300 in a German poem and then, in 1588, by Johann Fischart. While on the way to mass, Peter encountered a beauteous maiden sitting on a rock. She told him that she had long been waiting for him and was in love with him, and she promised to live with him and bring him honor and good fortune if he promised never to marry another woman. Many years later, at the insistence of the Emperor, Peter became engaged to the latter's niece, thus breaking his promise. When he persisted, despite warnings, in marrying the lady, he died, just as his first beloved had predicted he would.

The hurdy-gurdy girl/baker boy episode was probably inspired by an anecdote related by Martin Zeiller in one of his commentaries to his translations of Francois Rosset's *Theatrum tragicum (Herrn Frantzen von Rosset Wunderlich und Trawrige Geschichten. . . .* Ulm: Johann Görlin, 1655, p. 20):

Anno 1625 I read a written *consilium* of a learned man well known to me (but now dead) of whom a clergyman had sought advice about how he should treat a young soldier who had revealed to him, the clergyman, that for a long time he had been having relations with a woman who sometimes disappeared, sometimes came back again, and was living with him as his concubine. She was not opposed to church service and sometimes urged him to pray, and considered him her husband, and did not wish to permit him to marry another; and she received him lovingly and claimed that by marrying him she might be freed of some strange curses and become a complete human being. She did not in any way prevent him from taking communion or from other Christian practices, but rather comported herself in such fashion that he could not hold her to be a devil.

In the same commentary Zeiller mentions both the Melusina and the Peter von Stauffenberg legends.

3. *astounded that no money had been found:* the search for the missing money leads its owner, the merchant-narrator of *The Wondrous Bird's Nest, Part II,* to the possession of the bird's nest.

CHAPTER 27

1. *one of the halberdiers:* the young man, who disappeared because he had picked up the magic bird's nest dropped by the hurdy-gurdy girl, becomes the narrator of the next of the Simplician novels, *The Wondrous Bird's Nest, Part I.*

2. *the Rhine had swept away the bridge:* this apparently superfluous event in fact identified for Grimmelshausen's contemporaries both the scene and the time of the meeting of Philarchus, Simplicissimus, and Hopalong. It was well known that the St. Stephen's bridge across the Rhine at Strasbourg was nearly swept away in January 1670. Johann Jakob Walther (d. after 1679), painter, city councillor, and chronicler of Strasbourg, noted the following in his chronicle for 1670: "Toward the end of the year [1669 is meant] such a bitter cold had begun that all waters, even the Rhine, were completely frozen over.... Saturday, 9 January a terrible spectacle could be seen here, when at St. Stephen's Bridge ice was piled up as high as a man (because it couldn't drift any further).... Last night the ice tore away and completely ruined 18 spans on the Rhine bridge. Half the town ran out to see this terrible event" (quoted in Franciscus Reisseisen, *Strassburger Chronik von 1657–1677,* p. 85, footnotes 1 and 2).

   News of this catastrophe spread over the German-speaking area. The *Theatrum Europaeum* took note of it in a section which dealt with natural catastrophes which occurred in 1670: "In Strasbourg a sudden onset of warm weather caused the Rhine to thaw and blocks of ice to flow down in such quantity that they tore away two spans on the small bridge and five on the long one and ruined almost completely ten others, a thing which had never been seen before."

Bibliography

A. GERMAN EDITIONS OF GRIMMELSHAUSEN'S WORKS

1. *Der seltzame Springinsfeld*
   Grimmelshausens Springinsfeld, Abdruck der ältesten Originalausgabe (1670) mit den Lesarten der andern zu Lebzeiten des Verfassers erschienenen Ausgabe. Edited by J. H. Scholte. ("Neudrucke deutscher Literaturwerke des XVI. und XVII. Jahrhunderts," Vols. 249-252.) Halle: Max Niemeyer Verlag, 1928.
   Der seltzame Springinsfeld. Edited by G. G. Sieveke. (Gesammelte Werke in Einzelausgaben.) Tübingen: H. Niemeyer, 1969.

2. Works
   Hans Jacob Christoffels von Grimmelshausen Simplicianische Schriften. Edited by Heinrich Kurz. ("Deutsche Bibliothek," Vols. 3-6.) Leipzig: J. J. Weber, 1863-64.
   Grimmelshausens Werke. Edited by Felix Bobertag. ("Deutsche National-Litteratur," Vols. 33-35.) Berlin and Stuttgart: W. Spemann, 1882-.
   Grimmelshausens Werke in 4 Teilen. Edited by H. H. Borcherdt. Berlin: Bong, 1921.
   Die Simplicianischen Schriften des Hans Jacob Christoffel von Grimmelshausen. Monumentalausgabe in zwei Bänden. Edited by Franz Riederer. Naunhof bei Leipzig: F. W. Hendel, 1939.
   Der abenteuerliche Simplicissimus and *Simplicianische Schriften.* Edited by Alfred Kelletat. ("Werke der Weltliteratur in Dünndruckausgaben," Vols. 21 and 41.) Munich: Winckler, 1956/1958.
   Grimmelshausens Werke in vier Bänden. Edited by Siegfried Streller. Berlin and Weimar: Aufbau Verlag, 1960.

B. WORKS CITED IN THE NOTES

Garzoni, Tomaso. *Piazza universale, Das ist: Allgemeiner Schauplatz / oder Marckt / und Zusammenkunfft aller Professionen / Künsten / Geschäfften / Händeln und Handwercken / so in der gantzen Welt geübet werden....* Frankfurt am Main: Lucas Jennesius, 1626.
Grimmelshausens Springinsfeld.... Edited by J. H. Scholte. (Cf. Section A)
Guevara, Antonio de. *Von Beschwerligkeit und Uberdruss des Hofflebens und Lob dess Feldbaws oder Landsitzes....* Lübeck: Lorentz Albrecht Bürger, 1600.
Haberkamm, Klaus. *"Sensus Astrologicus." Zum Verhältnis von Literatur und Astrologie in Renaissance und Barock.* ("Abhandlungen zur Kunst-, Musik-, und Literaturwissenchaft," Vol. 124.) Bonn: Bouvier, 1972.

Handwörterbuch des deutschen Aberglaubens. Edited by Hanns Bächtold-Stäubli et al. 10 vols. Berlin and Leipzig: W. de Gruyter & Co., 1927–42.

Klein, Mary L. *Johann Jacob Christoffel von Grimmelshausen's 'Satyrischer Pilgrim,' A Critical Edition with Introduction and Notes.* Unpublished Ph.D. Dissertation, University of Texas, 1963.

Könnecke, Gustav. *Quellen und Forschungen zur Lebensgeschichte Grimmelshausens.* Edited by J. H. Scholte. 2 vols. Weimar: Gesellschaft der Bibliophilen, 1926.

Koschlig, Manfred. *Grimmelshausen und seine Verleger.* ("Palaestra," Vol. 218.) Leipzig: Akademische Verlagsgesellschaft m. b. H., 1939.

Lauremberg, Peter. *Acerra philologica. Das ist: Vierhundert ausserlesene Nützliche, lustige und denckwürdige Historien und Discursen....* Leyden: Frantz Heger, 1646.

Moscherosch, Hans Michael. *Visiones de Don de Quevedo. Das ist: Wunderliche Satirische und warhafftige Gesichte Philanders von Sittewald....* Frankfurt: Johann Gottfried Schönwetter, 1645–48.

Peuckert, Will Erich. "Zu Grimmelshausens 'Springinsfeld,'" *Zeitschrift für deutsche Philologie,* Vol. 74 (1955). Pp. 422–23.

Reisseisen, Franciscus. *Strassburgische Chronik von 1657–1677.* Edited by Rudolf Reuss. Strasbourg: C. F. Schmidt, 1888.

Rosset, François. *Herrn Frantzen von Rosset Wunderlich und Trawrige Geschichten. Durch Martin Zeillern Auss dem Frantzösischen verteütscht...* (earlier versions were entitled *Theatrum Tragicum*). Ulm: Johann Görlin, 1655.

Scholte, J. H. *Zonagri Discurs von Waarsagern. Ein Beitrag zu unserer Kenntnis von Grimmelshausens Arbeitsweise....* ("Verhandelingen der koninklijke Akademie van Wetenschappen te Amsterdam, Afdeeling Letterkunde," New Series, Vol. 22.) Amsterdam: Johannes Müller, 1921.

Die Simplicianischen Schriften.... Edited by Franz Riederer. (Cf. Section A)

Sutherland, C. V. H. *English Coinage 600–1900.* London: B. T. Batsford Ltd., 1973.

Theatrum Europaeum.... 6 parts. Frankfurt am Main: Wolfgang Hoffman, 1646–52.

Theatrum Europaeum.... 20 parts. Frankfurt am Main: various publishers, 1662–1734.

Wassenberg, Eberhard. *Der ernewerte Teutsche Florus Eberhard Wassenbergs mit Animadversionen, Additionen und Correctionen....* Amsterdam: Ludwig Elzevier, 1647.

Weydt, Günther. *Nachahmung und Schöpfung im Barock.* Bern and Munich: Francke Verlag, 1968.

Robert L. Hiller and John C. Osborne are professors of German at the University of Tennessee, Knoxville. Hiller holds the Ph.D. degree from Cornell University, Osborne the Ph.D. degree from Northwestern University. They previously collaborated on a translation of *The Runagate Courage,* the second of the Simplician novels.

The manuscript was edited by Jean Spang. The book was designed by Edgar Frank. The typeface for the text is Times Roman, based on a design by Stanley Morison in 1931. The display type is Garamond. The book is printed on Booktext Natural paper and bound on Holliston Mills' Kingston Natural Finish cloth over binder's boards. Manufactured in the United States of America.